AUTHOR

This GCSE guide was written by Kerry Lewis, author of Amazon best sellers *Mr Grammar* and *Mr Bruff's Guide to A' Level English Literature*. Kerry has also written *Mr Bruff's Guide to Jane Eyre* and co-written Mr Bruff guides to *The Tempest* and *Julius Caesar*.

She been a member of the mrbruff.com team since May 2014. You can follow her on Twitter @Mrs_SPaG.

DEDICATIONS

Kerry Lewis would like to thank Andrew Simmons for his hard work and good-natured willingness with editing this book. She would also like to thank history expert Julie Boden for casting her eyes over the contextual information.

Mr Bruff would like to thank Sunny Ratilal and Sam Perkins, who designed the front cover of this eBook.

COPYRIGHT

The entire text is copyright © 2018 by Kerry Lewis. No part of this book may be reproduced, duplicated or transmitted by either electronic means or in printed format without written permission of the publisher. All rights reserved.

FREE EBOOK

Email info@mrbruff.com with proof of purchase, and we will send you a free eBook edition of this revision guide.

Introduction

Initially, British publishers refused to accept *Animal Farm* for publication because it is critical of the rise of communism in the Soviet Union. At this stage of the second world war, the Soviet Union was a necessary support for the Allies in their fight against Hitler and Nazi Germany. Publishing the novella might therefore cause offence. From the beginning, the novella therefore had the power to influence opinion.

Animal Farm was finally published in the UK on 17 August 1945; a year later, it was published in America and it became an immediate success—increasingly so from 1947 when the Cold War began in earnest. The American and European political climates were now ready for a novella that challenged the political philosophy of communism.

The novella was originally called *Animal Farm: A Fairy Story*, yet beneath the story of the talking animals are many other layers of meaning. Contemporary and modern readers can examine and understand how the Communist Party rose to power in Russia. However, this is not just the story of the rise of a particular political party. It is a story about the corruption and abuse of power in all totalitarian regimes—and, as Orwell saw it, their inevitable tyranny, manipulation and betrayal of individuals and their original ideals. These ideas are just as politically relevant today as they were in the twentieth century.

This GCSE revision guide aims to lead you through the key themes of the novella, linking them to context, and analysing language, form and structure.

It is worth mentioning that, in addition to his wide range of revision guides, Mr Bruff has a flourishing YouTube channel with hundreds of videos focusing on GCSE English language and English literature as well as the A' levels in English literature and language. His videos have been viewed over 20 million times across 198 nations—sample them on https://www.youtube.com/user/mrbruff. Mr Bruff can be contacted at info@mrbruff.com.

I hope you find this revision guide useful!

Kerry Lewis

@Mrs_SPaG

Contents

Useful Vocabulary 5

The Author: George Orwell 6

Title, Form and Genre 8
    Plot Recap 8
    Title 8
    Form 9
    Allegory 9
    Fairy Story 10
    Political Satire 10

Animal Farm and Historical Parallels 11
    Chapter 1 11
    Chapter 2 13
    Chapter 3 14
    Chapter 4 15
    Chapter 5 15
    Chapter 6 16
    Chapter 7 17
    Chapter 8 18
    Chapter 9 19
    Chapter 10 20

Symbolism of Setting 21
    The Farm 21
    The Barn 21
    Windmill 22

Structure 23
    Freytag's Pyramid 23
    Chronological Structure 25
    Cyclical Structure 25
    Foreshadowing 26

Language 26

Simplicity	26
Irony	26
Humour	27
Motifs	28
THEME: The Power of Language	32
Old Major's Speech	32
Squealer	34
Minimus	37
Moses and Religion	37
THEME: Revolution	38
The Key Players	38
Napoleon	39
Snowball	39
Power Struggles	40
THEME: Tyranny, the Abuse of Power and Corruption of Animalism	41
Mr and Mrs Jones	41
The Pigs	42
Pigs as Men	47
THEME: Class Structures	48
Benjamin	49
Boxer	49
Cat	50
Clover	50
Dogs	50
Major	51
Mollie	51
Muriel	51
Pigeons	51
Sheep	52
THEME: International Alliances	52
Useful Quotations	53
Example essay	60

Useful Vocabulary

Throughout the twentieth century, the country that initially called itself the Russian Empire changed its name two more times. A brief explanation follows.

What was Russia Called?

The country that today we call Russia was once known as the **Russian Empire**, ruled by Tsar Nicholas II from 1896. Then, in 1917, there were two revolutions.

Following the February revolution, the Provisional Government of mainly capitalists and the aristocracy replaced the tsar, who abdicated. With the October revolution, the Bolsheviks, led by Lenin, seized control and overthrew the Provisional Government. Between 1922-1991, the Russian Empire became the **Soviet Union**, or **USSR** (Union of Soviet Socialist Republic), and it expanded to fifteen states. The Soviet Union was dissolved 1991 and is now known as **Russia.**

The people who fought for a communist Russia were called **Bolsheviks**; they were members of the Russian Social Democratic Party. Their revolutionary **Red Army**, sometimes called the Reds, was established after the October 1917 Revolution (also called Red October), and it consisted of workers and peasants. In contrast, the **White Army** (or the Whites) was anti-Bolshevik.

In your exam, if you are discussing the farm under the ownership of Mr Jones at the beginning of the novella and want to talk about context, reference the Russian Empire. Once the animals seize control, reference the Soviet Union (or the USSR).

Political Words

With the changing political climate of nineteenth- and twentieth-century Europe, there evolved new words to describe emerging political systems or ideologies. Some of these new words are below, alongside other words that might be useful for understanding *Animal Farm*.

Anarchism: a political philosophy that believes that all governments should be abolished, and that people should choose to work together to govern themselves without compulsion. ***Anarchist:*** a person who supports this philosophy.

Capitalism: a political system in which a country's trade and industry are controlled by private owners for profit, rather than by the state.

Communism: a society in which property is owned by the community rather than individuals. Each person is equal, contributing according to their ability and receiving according to their needs. ***Communist:*** a person who supports this society.

Dictatorship: a system of rule in which a society is run by a dictator, who has total power. Everything that the dictator says is law and must be obeyed.

Fascism: a governmental system that is frequently led by a dictator having complete power, forcibly suppressing opposition, regimenting all industry, commerce, etc. A fascist government is aggressively nationalistic and often racist.

KGB: the Russian secret police whose purpose is to eliminate any opposition. The KGB started in the 1950s. From 1917, the secret police were known as the Cheka. Under Stalin, they were called the NKVD.

Left wing (noun): a political party with socialist tendencies. It aims to reform and might have radical views. (Adjective: ***left-wing***.)

Marxism: a political ideology based on the ideas of Karl Marx and Friedrich Engels. It is a philosophical framework used to create a communist state. This will be discussed in more detail later in this guide.

Republic: a state (for example, the USA) in which the people have the power and they are led by an elected president.

Right wing (noun): conservatives (people who are reluctant to change because they like things as they are) and nationalists (people who think their nation's interests are more important than those of other nations). There are also ***far-right*** fascists and racists, who hold extreme right-wing beliefs.

Socialism: socialism and communism are often confused. According to Marxist theory, a socialist state is a state that is in transition: it has overthrown capitalism but has not yet fully achieved communism.

Totalitarianism: a form of government where a ruler (dictator) or a ruling group has complete control. This includes total control of the economy, media and the people.

The Author: George Orwell

George Orwell (1903-1950) is the pen name of Eric Arthur Blair, a novelist, essayist, critic and journalist, who was born in British India where his father worked in the Civil Service. When Orwell was one, his mother brought him and his two sisters to live in England.

Despite his great-great grandmother marrying an earl, his parents did not own any property and were dependent on the civil service for an income. This meant that they could not afford to send him to a public school (a selective, fee-paying independent school without financial support). Orwell was a bright child, and he won a partial scholarship to a preparatory school in Eastbourne where he boarded for five years. A budding writer, he composed two poems that were published in the local paper. At school, his awareness of the class system increased when he noticed that the richer students were treated better than the poorer ones. Hating his time at St. Cyprian's, he successfully won scholarships for Wellington College and for Eton. He attended Wellington in spring 1917 until a place became available at Eton where he was much happier. At Eton, he helped to produce the college magazine and other publications. His school experiences developed his awareness of class divisions in society.

When he left school, Orwell joined the India Imperial Police Force and in 1922 was posted to Burma. He had always been an independent thinker, so he learnt fluent Burmese; however, the better he got to know the native people, the more he felt guilty about his role in a British Empire colony. In *Animal Farm*, Mr Jones and the pigs exploit and maltreat the weak in the same way that some British colonisers exploited and maltreated the Burmese. His first novel *Burmese Days* (published in 1934) is based on his experiences in Burma and bitterly describes British prejudice and corruption. We therefore see that Orwell did not share contemporary beliefs about the benefits of colonialism: the concept of abusing power is a universal theme, not just limited to communist Russia. At this point, we can understand why, by the late 1920s, Orwell considered himself an anarchist (someone who does not recognise government authority).

In 1927, Orwell became very ill with the mosquito-borne dengue fever, so he returned home to England on leave. At this point, he decided to leave the Imperial Police to become a writer.

The next stage of Orwell's life is described in *Down and Out in Paris and London*, published in 1933. In his memoir, Orwell describes how, disguised as a tramp, he explored the poorer parts of London. He got to know its inhabitants and made notes about his experiences. He also spent two years in Paris where he continued to write, supporting himself by taking low-paid jobs such as dishwashing, which he describes in his book. He also wrote articles about unemployment and the social conditions of the poor—the theme of poverty was emerging as a deeply interesting subject for him.

When *Down and Out in Paris and London* was published, Orwell chose to publish under the *nom de plume* George Orwell because he did not want to embarrass his family about his time as a tramp.

Upon his return to England, Orwell wrote articles and novels, supporting himself with a range of jobs, including teaching, and working in a second-hand bookshop. He continued his occasional explorations, disguised as a tramp, and did low-paid jobs that provided material for his writing. At one point, Orwell unsuccessfully tried to get himself arrested in the hope that he would be sent to prison, so that he could write about the experience!

His novel *A Clergyman's Daughter* was published in 1935; and *Keep the Aspidistra Flying* was published in 1936.

In 1936, Orwell accepted a commission to write about social conditions in the north of England. He spent a month in Wigan, visiting the poor, investigating how they lived and worked—he saw first-hand the effects of overwork and hunger later described in *Animal Farm*. As well as visiting coal mines, he attended meetings of the Communist Party (and formed a low opinion of Oswald Mosley, leader of the British Union of Fascists). Orwell's experiences culminated in *The Road to Wigan Pier*, published in 1937. The first half describes his investigations while the second half is a controversial essay in which he describes his middle-class background and the development of his political conscience. At this point, he considered himself to be a socialist and challenged British attitudes towards socialism.

Orwell's political views were so strong that, at the end of 1936 (the same year that he married Eileen O'Shaughnessy), he decided to go to Spain to fight in the Spanish Civil War. He wanted to defend the left-wing Republican government against General Franco, the fascist leader supported by Hitler.

In Spain, Orwell fought alongside members of an anti-Stalinist movement. He saw active service and survived being shot in the throat by a sniper. When he was in Barcelona, the situation began to deteriorate, as Soviet-backed communists began to suppress their political opponents, who included socialists. The communist press spread lies and propaganda, accusing the anti-Stalinists of collaborating with the fascists. (The use of propaganda can be seen through the character of Squealer in *Animal Farm*.) Consequently, Orwell and Eileen were forced to flee Spain in fear of their lives. Orwell's experiences in the Spanish Civil War and his disillusionment with the Communist Party are described in *Homage to Catalonia*, published in 1938. Orwell now hated any form of totalitarianism: socialism, communism or fascism. These views form the underlying ideology of *Animal Farm* and his final novel *Nineteen Eighty-Four*.

With the outbreak of World War II, Orwell was declared unfit for military service by the Medical Board because of the condition of his lungs, so from 1941 to 1943, he worked for the BBC's Eastern Service, countering Nazi propaganda. (It was around this time that he started to write *Animal Farm*.)

In November 1943, Orwell became literary editor of the Tribune. His literary output as a journalist became prolific: he wrote numerous reviews and articles.

It is at this point that we can appreciate the significance of the political context. We already know how Orwell's life helped to shape his views and that *Animal Farm* was an attack on the Soviet regime. British politics of the time also impacted on Orwell's life: initially, publishers refused to accept *Animal Farm: A Fairy Story* because the Soviet Union was a war ally. In 1945, the year the war ended, and Eileen died, the novella was finally published in the UK. A year later, it was published in America and became an immediate success—increasingly so from 1947 when the Cold War began.

Now a well-known writer, Orwell mixed journalism with contributions to literary magazines. He worked on his last and possibly most famous novel *Nineteen Eighty-Four*, which was published in June 1949.

Suffering from tuberculosis, Orwell married Sonia Brownell from his hospital bed in October 1949. Three months later, he died at the age of 46.

Title, Form and Genre

Plot Recap

At Manor Farm, a pig called Major tells the animals about Animalism and, shortly afterwards, he dies. The drunken farmer Mr Jones forgets to feed the animals, which triggers a rebellion. The animals decide to live by the ideas of Animalism, which the pigs summarise as the Seven Commandments. The pigs, led by Napoleon and Snowball, take charge, and the animals successfully win the Battle of the Cowshed against the returning humans. Napoleon sets his dogs on his rival Snowball, who flees the farm. Napoleon, assisted by Squealer's propaganda, consolidates his position and becomes a dictator. One by one, the commandments are broken by the pigs. The animals' lives become harder: they work like slaves; there is less food; Napoleon starves the hens to death; there are forced confessions and executions. Minimus encourages the animals to view Napoleon as a cult figure. Napoleon forges a trade alliance with a neighbouring farmer, which results in the Battle of the Windmill. Eventually, Boxer the hard-working horse is taken away by the knacker, but the animals believe the pigs' lies, so we see that the pigs' power and control is absolute. At the end of the novella, the pigs have the same status as humans, and the animals' lives are just as bad—if not worse—than they were under Mr Jones.

Title

Wanting a fresh start after the revolution, the animals get rid of the name of Manor Farm, which reminds them too much of Mr Jones. In the allegory, Manor Farm represents the Russian Empire, a totalitarian feudal country ruled by Mr Jones's historical counterpart, Tsar Nicholas II.

The name change to Animal Farm parallels the historical name change to the Soviet Union (USSR) under communist rule. Animal Farm represents the idealistic hopes and dreams of the animals, a haven where they are equal and free from totalitarian rule, just as the Soviet Union represented the communist ideology of everyone being equal. The title *Animal Farm* is therefore a metaphor for communism in the Soviet Union (this is discussed in more detail in **Allegory**, below). This metaphor can be extended to all human societies in which totalitarian regimes rise to power.

At the end of the novella, the pigs change the name of the farm back to Manor Farm. This symbolises the cyclical nature of tyranny, as the farm has now become the totalitarian regime against which the animals initially rebelled. The animals will continue to be exploited, and they will work until they can work no more. Orwell therefore manipulates the title to encourage the reader to reflect upon the hypocrisies of the communist regime.

FORM

Orwell opted to write the novella (short novel) in the third person (using *he, she, it* and *they*) to deliberately distance the reader from events. For example, the reader is first alerted to the hypocrisy of the pigs when in chapter 2 'it was noticed that the milk had disappeared'. The use of the passive voice creates a neutral tone and emphasises how the animals notice the absence of the milk yet draw no conclusions as to where it has gone. By presenting the animals' perspective, the reader is encouraged to judge the characters and their actions, forming an independent conclusion as to what is really happening. Through his use of the passive voice, Orwell therefore draws the reader's attention to the way the pigs (and by implication all leaders of communist states) manipulate power for their own selfish ends.

Another benefit of telling the story from the perspective of the animals is that it fits communist ideology: it focuses on the workers and their experience of Animalism. This narrative choice heightens the irony at the end of the novella. Even in as late as chapter 10, the animals still naïvely believe that 'All animals are equal' and they still believe that they are working for a better life. This optimism contrasts with the pigs' totalitarian rule, heightening the impact of the final scene in the chapter when the animals are wholly unable to distinguish the pigs from the humans.

ALLEGORY

As we have seen, the novella was written in World War II when the Soviet Union and Britain were allies in the struggle against Hitler. We also know that Orwell was anti-communist because of his experiences in Spain. Orwell therefore aimed to criticise the Soviet Union indirectly. In order to do this, he took the form or genre of a fable (a short story with animal characters and a moral) and expanded it into an allegory.

An allegory is a fable or story that is an extended metaphor: it has another meaning beyond the obvious surface meaning. On the surface, *Animal Farm* is a story about Napoleon's rise to power on the farm. In reality, the novella is a metaphor for Stalin's equally ruthless rise to power in the Soviet Union. This is a clever choice of genre not least because it enables Orwell to make the complex world of communist politics accessible to the everyday reader.

For example, we associate particular animals with well-known character traits: horses are hard-working, sheep lack intelligence, and dogs can be vicious. Orwell uses these traits as vehicles for his characters and their links to communism. For example, Napoleon is a pig, and pigs connote laziness and greed. Perhaps another layer of meaning is that the pigs symbolise all greedy exploitative tyrants in any country. This makes the story simpler and helps the reader to understand the dangers that communism presents.

Orwell also invites us to think about the gullible and apathetic populace who allow these regimes to emerge. His choice of the allegory form therefore encourages the reader to explore a range of meanings.

FAIRY STORY

The original name of the novella was *Animal Farm: A Fairy Story*. Let's explore some elements of a fairy story:

ELEMENTS OF A FAIRY STORY	*ANIMAL FARM* EVIDENCE
SET IN THE PAST	Use of past tense
FANTASY ELEMENTS	The animals can talk
	The pigs can walk on two legs
TRADITIONAL GOOD VERSUS EVIL CHARACTERS	Good—old Major and his theory of Animalism. He wants to defeat the evil Mr Jones
	Good—Snowball tries to defeat Napoleon
	Evil—Mr Jones and Napoleon

Many fairy tales begin with a functioning, well-ordered setting, so the reader of *Animal Farm* begins the novella expecting that everything at Manor Farm will be secure. This heightens the shock when we meet Mr Jones (or Tsar Nicholas II) in the first paragraph—more on this later in the guide.

Furthermore, fairy tales generally adhere to a particular structure: there is a clearly defined problem which comes to a climax, the problem is solved, and everyone lives happily ever after. The readers of *Animal Farm* would have expected a similar ending so, when this does not happen, the shock is considerable. Communist rule under Lenin and Stalin promised benefits to the Russian people—benefits that were not delivered; instead, communism created misery and inequality. Orwell might be suggesting that Marxism is like a fairy tale: it promises good things but cannot deliver. The reality of the unhappy ending in the novella in Orwell's view is proven by events in the real world. The title's reference to a fairy tale is thus deliberately deceptive: it seduces the reader into expecting a happy ending which does not happen, heightening the impact of his message about the dangers of communism.

Interestingly, when *Animal Farm* was published in America, publishers dropped the *Fairy Tale* part of the title because it was obvious that the novella was not a traditional story for children. Translations of the novella into other languages followed suit and left out the *Fairy Tale* wording; however, in some editions, publishers added the subtitle *A Satire* or *A Contemporary Satire* to make the critical purpose of the novella as obvious as possible. Original Fairy Tale subtitle notwithstanding, it is clear that the novella is and has always been a work of political satire.

POLITICAL SATIRE

What is satire exactly? A satire is a literary or other artistic work that ridicules the vices, silliness and shortcomings of people, organisations, government or society. Orwell uses the novella to ridicule the myth of communism. Depicting Stalin as a pig and many other characters as animals turns them into objects of ridicule.

Orwell uses irony (see **Language**, below) to create satire and exaggerate the faults of the pigs.

ANIMAL FARM AND HISTORICAL PARALLELS

Animal Farm mirrors events leading up to the overthrow of Tsar Nicholas (Mr Jones) after the 1917 Russian Revolution led by Lenin. Then the novella takes us through the 1918-1921 Russian Civil War (Battle of the Cowshed) and into the period after Lenin's death in 1924 when Stalin (Napoleon) took complete control of the reins of power. Stalin was a mass murderer on a scale beyond even Hitler: historians estimate that he was responsible for the deaths of between 6 to 20 million people.

With each chapter summary of *Animal Farm* below, historical parallels are drawn. Please note that events in the novella do not always reflect the chronology of historical events.

CHAPTER 1

Animal Farm:	Mr Jones, the drunken owner of Manor Farm, falls asleep.
Historical parallel:	From the early 1900s, the Russian people were increasingly unhappy with Tsar Nicholas II's poor leadership. Like the tsar, Mr Jones was irresponsible and out of touch. Mr Jones's drunkenness symbolises the tsar's inadequacy.
Animal Farm:	The pig 'old Major' delivers a rousing speech about Animalism.
Historical parallel:	The founding fathers of communism, Karl Marx (1818–1883) and Friedrich Engels (1820-1895), published their thoughts in a *Communist Manifesto* (1848). These two German political philosophers conceived of communism as an economic and social system in which all property and resources are owned by the state on behalf of everyone.
Animal Farm:	Old Major's speech about 'Animalism' reflects many aspects of communist ideology; the pig's hatred for 'Man' might also mirror Lenin's hatred of the tsar and his family (it is a widely-held belief that Lenin gave the order for their assassination). Major's speech is analysed in more detail later in this guide, so here is a summary of the key points and their links to the *Communist Manifesto*:

'Animalism' Ideology in Old Major's Speech	Communist Ideology in the *Communist Manifesto*
The animals are miserable and exploited: 'the life of an animal is misery and slavery'.	All historical developments are because of class struggles in which the ruling classes defeat and exploit the workers.
'Remove man from the scene, and the root cause of hunger and overwork is abolished for ever'.	With no ruling class, the populace collectively owns property and resources, so everyone has enough: 'From each according to his abilities, to each according to his needs'.
'Man is the only creature that consumes without producing'	Capitalists consume the profits yet (unlike the workers) do nothing to create them.
The animals should revolt against humans: 'Rebellion!'	This will only happen if there is a revolution: 'The proletarians [common workers] have nothing to lose but

		their chains. They have a world to win. Workers of the world, Unite!'
Describes a society where 'All animals are equal.'		Describes a society in which work and profits are shared equally. The social hierarchy, with its divisions between the rich and poor, is swept away.
Animal Farm:	Major teaches the animals 'Beasts of England'.	
Historical parallel:	The anthem 'Beasts of England' corresponds to the Soviet Union's national anthem, The Internationale. The words for anthem were written by left-wing French Revolutionary Eugène Edine Pottie in 1871, and the anthem, which is worth comparing with 'Beasts of England', was used by many left-wing organisations.	

The Internationale	No more deluded by reaction
	On tyrants only we'll make war
Arise ye workers from your slumbers	The soldiers too will take strike action
Arise ye prisoners of want	They'll break ranks and fight no more
For reason in revolt now thunders	And if those cannibals keep trying
And at last ends the age of cant.	To sacrifice us to their pride
Away with all your superstitions	They soon shall hear the bullets flying
Servile masses arise, arise	We'll shoot the generals on our own side.
We'll change henceforth the old tradition	
And spurn the dust to win the prize.	No saviour from on high delivers
	No faith have we in prince or peer
Refrain:	Our own right hand the chains must shiver
So comrades, come rally	Chains of hatred, greed and fear
And the last fight let us face	E'er the thieves will out with their booty
The Internationale unites the human race.	And give to all a happier lot.
	Each at the forge must do their duty
	And we'll strike while the iron is hot.

Animal Farm:	Their singing wakes Mr Jones, who thinks there is a fox and fires his gun.	
Historical parallel:	The firing of the gun might symbolise how Tsar Nicholas II was associated with violence and death. His political opponents called him Nicholas the Bloody. Here are some reasons: • Khodynka Tragedy (1896): at a celebration of the crowning of the emperor and empress, 1,389 people were trampled to death and roughly the same number again were injured. • Anti-Semitic pogroms (organised massacres of Jews) 1903-1906: the tsar was responsible for the estimated deaths of up to 2,500 Jews. • Bloody Sunday or Red Sunday (1905): The Imperial Guard fired upon unarmed demonstrators, as they marched towards the Winter Palace in St. Petersburg to present a petition to Tsar Nicholas II of Russia. About 200 people died and 800 were wounded. • After the unsuccessful 1905 Revolution: the number of death sentences and executions dramatically increased. • Russo-Japanese War (1904-5): the tsar was widely believed to be responsible for this war. The Japanese victors destroyed the Russian fleet and won every battle.	

Chapter 2

Animal Farm:	**Major dies. He does not see the animals' rebellion.**
Historical parallel:	Karl Marx died in 1883, aged 64. Friedrich Engels died in 1895, aged 75. Neither of them lived long enough to see the Russian Revolution.
Animal Farm:	The pigs teach the animals about Major's ideology, which they call 'Animalism'. The animals plan a rebellion.
Historical parallel:	Socialist ideas from the *Communist Manifesto* spread across Europe. Lenin became actively involved in the socialist movement. (NB: the terms Marxism or communism were used interchangeably.)
Animal Farm:	Not everyone supports Animalism: • Mollie is reluctant to join in. • Moses the raven is also suspicious, and Moses is not seen again.
Historical parallel:	• Mollie represents the bourgeois (the middle classes) who valued their possessions and money. • Moses symbolises the Russian Orthodox Church, which supported the Russian monarchy. The church was regarded as too independent and a threat to the communist movement, so Stalin persecuted organised religion, defiling churches and executing priests.
Animal Farm:	Boxer and Clover are the greatest supporters of the rebellion.
Historical parallel:	Boxer and Clover symbolise the working classes exploited under the tsar's rule. They immediately supported the revolution.
Animal Farm:	Mr Jones neglects the harvest to go to the local pub. On return, he falls drunkenly asleep, forgetting to feed the animals once again. In desperation, the animals break into the store-shed to find food. Mr Jones and his men attack the cows with whips, but the animals turn on them and chase them off the farm. The animals then destroy everything that reminds them of Mr Jones and his men.
Historical parallel:	Because of his poor military leadership and mismanagement, Tsar Nicolas II was responsible for millions of unnecessary deaths in the Russian armies and terrible food shortages at home. The 1917 Russian Revolution began in February with violent riots, which saw the tsar removed from power. Later, in October, the Bolsheviks (a faction of the Social Democratic Labour Party) seized power and declared Vladimir Lenin their leader.
Animal Farm:	The animals celebrate. They explore the farm and Mr Jones's house. They are stunned by the luxury in which he lived and decide firstly to preserve the farmhouse as a museum to illustrate the evils of inequality and secondly to stipulate that no animal shall ever live there in the comfort that Mr Jones enjoyed.
Historical parallel:	The storming of the Tsar's Winter Palace in St. Petersburg, after which it was declared a museum.
Animal Farm:	Snowball paints 'Animal Farm' on the gate and then paints the 'Seven Commandments' of Animalism on the wall of the barn.

Historical parallel:	In 1922, Lenin was elected chairman of the new government of the Soviet Union, or USSR (Union of Soviet Socialist Republics). Snowball is based on the charismatic revolutionary leader Trotsky. Many assumed he would lead the government after Lenin's death in 1924.
Animal Farm:	The pigs milk the cows, and the milk disappears.
Historical parallel:	This symbolises that in Orwell's view the ideology of communism is flawed and that the pigs are in it for themselves from the beginning.

CHAPTER 3

Animal Farm:	**The pigs become supervisors and the animals bring in the harvest, but the work is hard.**
Historical parallel:	New forced labour policies.
Animal Farm:	The animals have a new flag depicting a hoof and horn.
Historical parallel:	The communist flag with its hammer and sickle.
Animal Farm:	On Sundays, the animals meet and listen to Snowball and Napoleon debating. Snowball forms committees to promote the better understanding of Animalism. As a skilled communicator (like Trotsky), he helps the animals to understand Animalism by condensing its complicated message to the simple maxim: 'Four legs good, two legs bad'.
Historical parallel:	Trotsky and Stalin competed for power and influence. Trotsky set up committees—he was Lenin's chief organiser and facilitator.
Animal Farm:	Education for the animals continues.
Historical parallel:	In 1919, education for children was made compulsory. Literacy schools were set up for adults who could not read or write.
Animal Farm:	Napoleon takes Jessie and Bluebell's puppies away.
Historical parallel:	Primary and secondary schools focused on the principles of communism to create 'good' citizens. The children would leave school fully supportive of the communist regime.
Animal Farm:	The animals learn that the pigs have been consuming 'milk and apples', mixed in their mash. Squealer defends Napoleon.
Historical parallel:	Gradually, class divisions reappeared in the USSR, based on party membership, and some people became more important than others. To defend this, the activities of the Soviet propaganda machine increased.

Chapter 4

Animal Farm:	**Snowball and Napoleon send pigeons to neighbouring farms to teach the animals 'Beasts of England'.**
Historical parallel:	From 1924-1935, in the period after the White Russian forces had been defeated in the civil war, Trotsky encouraged a 'permanent world revolution' with the goal of global communism.
Animal Farm:	It's October. Mr Jones returns to Animal Farm, this time with some men. Snowball takes charge of the animals and drives the humans away. The animals celebrate 'The Battle of the Cowshed'.
Historical parallel:	The North Russia Intervention (1918-1920). The anti-revolutionary Allies (a multinational force) invaded the Soviet Union after the October Revolution, aiming to remove Lenin and the communist government from power. Trotsky mobilised, organised and led the Red Army to victory.

Chapter 5

Animal Farm:	**Mollie disappears and is later seen wearing ribbons and looking content.**
Historical parallel:	Disaffected White Russians emigrated from the Soviet Union in the years immediately after the Russian Revolution.
Animal Farm:	Snowball wants to build a windmill because of its long-term benefits. Napoleon objects, asserting that it is more important to produce food. The disagreements continue.
Historical parallel:	Tensions escalated between Trotsky and Stalin, as both men competed for power after the death of Lenin in 1924. Trotsky wanted to modernise the USSR (symbolised by Snowball's windmill) while Stalin wanted to focus on strengthening the Soviet Union.
Animal Farm:	Napoleon orders Jessie and Bluebell's puppies—now ferocious dogs—to run Snowball off the farm. We never see Snowball again.
Historical parallel:	Stalin forced Trotsky into exile where he was later assassinated. The dogs represent secret police agents, whose purpose was to eliminate any opposition at home or abroad.
Animal Farm:	Napoleon announces that the Sunday debates will stop and there will be new rules.
Historical parallel:	Stalin had total control: he was not interested in debates and new ideas.
Animal Farm:	Three weeks later, Napoleon declares, to everyone's surprise, that they will build the windmill.
Historical	The announcement of Stalin's Five-Year Plan to revitalise the Soviet Union's

parallel:	industry and agriculture.
Animal Farm:	The animals disinter old Major's skull and place it by the flagstaff and gun.
Historical parallel:	In 1924, Stalin ordered Lenin's body to be embalmed and put on public display.
Animal Farm:	Squealer explains that Snowball had stolen the plan for the windmill, and that it was originally Napoleon's idea.
Historical parallel:	The Soviet propaganda machine presented Stalin as a visionary leader and Trotsky as a traitor in the pay of the USSR's enemies.

CHAPTER 6

Animal Farm:	**Throughout the spring and summer, the animals work 'like slaves' to build the windmill.**
Historical parallel:	The start of Stalin's ambitious series of Five-Year Plans to modernise the Soviet Union, revitalising industry and agriculture. Stalin centralised command of the economy and industrialisation, transforming the Soviet Union into an industrial power and, in the process, causing huge suffering to the Russian people.
Animal Farm:	It is not easy to build the windmill, and Boxer works longer and harder than all the animals.
Historical parallel:	Gullible workers like Boxer believed in Stalin—this enabled him to retain power.
Animal Farm:	There are shortages of supplies that cannot be produced on the farm. Napoleon hires a solicitor, Mr. Whymper, to act as his agent because he wants to trade with neighbouring farms. There are rumours that he will trade with Pilkington or Frederick.
Historical parallel:	Mr Whymper represents the *Comintern*'s foreign agents. *Comintern* (the Communist International, also called the Third International) advocated world communism. As the novella unfolds, Pilkington will come to represent the Allies while Frederick will represent Hitler or Nazi Germany. This explains why they 'disliked each other' (see chapter 4).
Animal Farm:	Humans meet in pubs and discuss the state of the farm.
Historical parallel:	In 1933, the USA recognised the Soviet Union.
Animal Farm:	Squealer justifies to the animals the pigs' decision to move into the farmhouse.
Historical parallel:	Soviet propaganda.
Animal Farm:	In November, a storm destroys the unfinished windmill. Napoleon blames

	Snowball, putting a price on Snowball's head.
Historical parallel:	Many goals in Stalin's Five-Year Plans were unachievable. In Russia, Stalinist propaganda demonised the exiled Trotsky as an enemy of the state. He was accused of sabotage and betrayal: any problems to do with the Soviet Union were blamed on him.
Animal Farm:	Napoleon says that they will rebuild the windmill.
Historical parallel:	The Five-Year Plans continued.

CHAPTER 7

Animal Farm:	**Winter comes, and the animals run low on food.**
Historical parallel:	Stalin's centralised command of economy and industrialisation disrupted food production, resulting in extreme suffering.
Animal Farm:	Napoleon hoodwinks Mr. Whymper into thinking the animals have lots of food so that he can report this to other humans.
Historical parallel:	Under the Five-Year Plan, there were famines in which millions died. Stalin covered this up.
Animal Farm:	The hens do not want to give up their eggs, so Napoleon stops their rations and they starve to death.
Historical parallel:	From the late 1920s, Stalin began to seize land from the wealthier peasants (kulaks) to create collective farms. Many refused to give up their land. The subsequent disruption of Russian agriculture resulted in a famine between 1932-3. It is estimated that 20 million people died.
Animal Farm:	Napoleon announces plans to sell wood to Pilkington or Frederick. When he is about to sell to one farmer, he states that Snowball has been seen at the other man's farm and vice versa.
Historical parallel:	Before World War II, The Soviet Union played the Allies and the Germans off against each other when it was negotiating possible treaties.
Animal Farm:	Snowball is blamed for visiting the farm at night to sabotage their hard work. Squealer says that Snowball has sold himself to Frederick and has been Mr Jones's secret agent all along.
Historical parallel:	Anti-Trotsky propaganda.
Animal Farm:	Time passes, and it is now spring. Napoleon forces confessions from the animals who challenged him. Then his dogs kill them. Other animals confess to crimes and are killed.

Historical parallel:	The Great Purges, also known as the Great Terror, took place in the late 1930s. Stalin removed anyone he considered disloyal (including senior military and political figures) by putting them on trial, torturing them until they made false admissions of guilt and then executing them. Other opponents were exiled internally to Siberia or put to work in brutal prison camps.
Animal Farm:	The song 'Beasts of England' is banned because, being a revolutionary song, it is no longer relevant. Minimus teaches the animals a new song.
Historical parallel:	Stalin aimed to influence what people thought by making sure that writers, artists and musicians only produced work that was acceptable to him. The character of Minimus represents this attempt to manipulate public opinion.

CHAPTER 8

Animal Farm:	**Throughout the year, the animals work hard on the windmill but have less food to eat. Squealer tells them that despite appearances they are producing more food under Napoleon's rule.**
Historical parallel:	Soviet propaganda manipulates statistics to hoodwink and control the workers.
Animal Farm:	Minimus writes a poem, praising Napoleon.
Historical parallel:	State-sponsored committees and departments direct all forms of artistic self-expression to control people's thinking.
Animal Farm:	Executions continue.
Historical parallel:	1939 was the climax of the Great Terror, which by this stage was targeting ordinary people. Having eliminated all internal opposition, Stalin became a totalitarian dictator.
Animal Farm:	A cult of personality develops around Napoleon. On the rare occasions he appears in public, he is surrounded by ceremony: a gun is fired to celebrate his birthday; and the animals are expected to praise him (like people praise God) when good things happen.
Historical parallel:	Stalin used similar propaganda strategies.
Animal Farm:	The animals finish the windmill in August.
Historical parallel:	As a result of the Five-Year Plans, by 1937 there were significant improvements in the production of coal, oil, iron and electricity; however, conditions for the workers were still very bad.
Animal Farm:	The pigs enter negotiations to sell the wood to Frederick or Pilkington. There are more rumours, which are really propaganda.
Historical	Stalin's negotiations with Hitler and the Allies before World War II. When Stalin

parallel:	favoured one side, his propaganda would criticise the opposing side and vice versa.
Animal Farm:	Napoleon sells a pile of timber to Frederick. The latter, upon Napoleon's insistence, pays in cash. Whymper announces that the banknotes are forgeries. Napoleon passes the death sentence on Frederick.
Historical parallel:	Frederick represents Adolf Hitler. In 1939, he became Stalin's ally, and the two dictators agreed on a mutual Non-Aggression Pact between Germany and Russia. Two years later, however, Germany broke the pact and invaded Russia. The forged banknotes therefore symbolise lies.
Animal Farm:	The next morning, accompanied by a large group of men, Frederick attempts to take the farm by force. The humans blow up the windmill.
Historical parallel:	In 1941, Germany invaded Russia. The war destroyed much of the infrastructure of the Soviet Union between Moscow and the western borders.
Animal Farm:	The animals drive the men off the farm but suffer many deaths and injuries. Squealer tells the survivors that they have won 'The Battle of the Windmill'.
Historical parallel:	There are estimated to have been between 20-26 million Soviet casualties (dead and wounded) when Stalin's army defeated Hitler's on the Eastern Front.
Animal Farm:	Napoleon creates the Order of the Green Banner.
Historical parallel:	Stalin created the Order of Lenin.
Animal Farm:	A few days later, the pigs find a case of whisky in the cellar of the farmhouse. Napoleon drinks too much and the next day thinks he is dying, so he makes the drinking of alcohol punishable by death. When he has recovered from what was simply a hangover, Napoleon orders the animals' retirement home, a paddock, to be ploughed and planted with barley. Muriel notices that words have been added to the Fifth Commandment, which now reads 'No animal shall drink alcohol to excess'.
Historical parallel:	Napoleon's whisky drinking parallels Stalin's indifference to the welfare of his people. Stalin's attitude and lifestyle resembled that of the tsar he replaced. He continued to justify his actions through propaganda.

CHAPTER 9

Animal Farm:	**The animals begin to build a new windmill.**
Historical parallel:	After World War II, the Soviets rebuilt their infrastructure.
Animal Farm:	Contrary to the evidence of diminishing food supplies, Squealer tells the animals that they have more food than ever. While the animals have less to eat, the pigs become fatter. Napoleon fathers 31 piglets.

Historical parallel:	Despite the appalling 1946-7 famine, Stalin's grip on power increased.
Animal Farm:	In April, Animal Farm is proclaimed a republic and Napoleon its president.
Historical parallel:	In 1946, Stalin adopted the new title of Generalissimo of the Soviet Union, the highest military rank in the Soviet Union.
Animal Farm:	Moses returns.
Historical parallel:	After World War II, Stalin allowed the return of the Russian Orthodox Church. Stalin realised that religion was good for the totalitarian regime since it gave people hope and took their minds off their present anxieties.
Animal Farm:	Boxer, close to retirement, has been struggling with exhaustion and a split hoof, but he has continued to work very hard. One day he collapses, and Squealer tells the animals that a van is taking him to hospital. However, Benjamin can read the words on the side of the van, and he learns that it is a knacker's van. Boxer is too weak to escape, and the van drives away.
Historical parallel:	The Soviet Union exploited the agricultural labourers by ordering all land owned by individual peasants to be incorporated into huge, inefficient collective farms. Boxer's fate highlights the exploitation of the workers and the way the state trampled all over their individual rights.
Animal Farm:	Squealer tells the animals that the vet had bought a knacker's van but had not yet repainted the sign on the side. The animals believe him. A crate of whisky is delivered (presumably as a thank you for Boxer's carcass), and the pigs drink it all.
Historical parallel:	Stalin and followers used propaganda to control the populace, whom they exploited.

CHAPTER 10

Animal Farm:	**Years pass. Very few animals remember life before the rebellion. Mr Jones is dead, and many of the animals are either dead or, like Clover, past retirement age. However, no one is allowed to retire because, with the acquisition of Pilkington's fields, the farm is larger. There are now two windmills, and everyone but the pigs must work until they drop. The pigs continue to thrive, of course.**
Historical parallel:	In the years that follow World War II, the Soviet Union expanded into Eastern Europe. By 1949, it controlled all Eastern European governments except Yugoslavia.
Animal Farm:	One evening, Clover sees first Squealer and then other pigs walking on two legs. The slogan has now changed: 'Four legs good, two legs better!'. The Seven Commandments have been painted over and replaced with 'ALL ANIMALS ARE EQUAL / BUT SOME ANIMALS ARE MORE EQUAL THAN OTHERS'. The pigs wear clothes and carry whips.
Historical	Stalin and his inner circle lived the lifestyle of the former tsar.

parallel:	
Animal Farm:	The pigs give some neighbouring farmers a tour of the farm. After some speeches, the pigs and humans play cards but quarrel after drinking alcohol.
Historical parallel:	Tehran Conference, 1943: Stalin, Winston Churchill and Franklin D. Roosevelt met to discuss how they could ensure peace after the war. The argument symbolises that peace was not possible, hence the future Cold War.
Animal Farm:	Clover and the other animals look through the farmhouse windows and cannot tell which creatures are the humans and which are the pigs.
Historical parallel:	One totalitarian regime replaced another as the pigs replaced Jones: proof of the failure of communist ideology.

SYMBOLISM OF SETTING

THE FARM

As we have seen from the analysis of the title, Animal Farm is an extended metaphor for the Soviet Union (USSR) under the rule of the Communist Party. It comprises the ruling class of the pigs; the dogs, who are the law keepers or the secret police; and the other animals, who represent the workers. Like all countries, the farm has a national anthem, rituals and state holidays. The neighbouring farms represent the Allies and Germany.

Animal Farm does not represent just the Soviet Union, however. It represents any human society that has the potential for revolution and change.

THE BARN

The barn symbolises the collective memory of the new communist nation. Seven Commandments are painted on the wall, representing the founding ideology of the new regime. As the pigs consolidate their power, they break all the commandments by walking on two legs, wearing clothes, sleeping on beds, drinking alcohol and killing other animals. In the novella, we see that the animals accept how the pigs rewrite history because the gullible and dim-witted animals (except Benjamin and perhaps Muriel) struggle to remember what life was like before the changes. The revisions to the Commandments reveal the hypocrisy of the pigs. Eventually the Seven Commandments are reduced to 'ALL ANIMALS ARE EQUAL / BUT SOME ANIMALS ARE MORE EQUAL THAN OTHERS'. The final commandment consolidates the pigs' power: their power to rewrite history restricts the animals' sense of identity and status. By the end of the novella, they are completely dependent upon the pigs.

WINDMILL

The windmill has a variety of symbolic meanings, and these change as events in the novella unfold.

Initially, the windmill symbolises Snowball's plans to improve the life of the pigs; once Snowball is driven off the farm, however, it becomes a symbol of how Napoleon psychologically manipulates the animals and controls them for his own gain. At first, Napoleon opposes Snowball's plans for the windmill (his later change of mind reflects Stalin changing his mind after becoming a dictator when he introduced the first Five-Year Plan to modernise the Soviet Union's infrastructure). With his rhetorical skills, Squealer defends Napoleon from the suspicions of the animals just as the Soviet Union employed propaganda to justify Stalin's decisions.

The failure of the windmill in chapter 6 becomes a metaphor for the poor management skills of the pigs, who did not see the need for thicker walls. By extension, this is a metaphor for failures of the Soviet government. The collapse of the windmill parallels the world witnessing the industrial incompetence of the Soviets: Stalin's Five-Year plans for agriculture collapsed and resulted in millions of people starving to death. On the farm, the humans are watching the animals just as the world watched the struggling Soviet Union—the pigs conceal the declining food supplies just as the Soviet Union attempted to conceal their problems from the world. The windmill therefore becomes a yardstick by which to measure the success of Animalism; Animal Farm needs to show the world that the windmill and hence Animalism is a success if it is to be taken seriously by the outside world.

When the windmill first collapses, the pigs play on the idea of the windmill and the farm's enemies to control the animals. Snowball becomes a scapegoat; by blaming an external force, the pigs stop the animals from examining too closely the internal workings of the farm and questioning the pigs' competence. This mirrors Stalin's use of Trotsky, who came to symbolise enemy forces; this continued even after Stalin had Trotsky assassinated in Mexico. Squealer and Napoleon use Snowball to their own advantage to represent the pigs as the saviours of the animals. The storm's destruction of the windmill provides Napoleon with the opportunity to turn events to his advantage by positioning himself as a firm, decisive leader, and the windmill becomes an important symbol around which to unite the animals against a common enemy. At the same time, it symbolises the exploitation of the gullible animals.

In chapter 8, Napoleon attempts to use the windmill's symbolic significance to boost his public image by naming it 'Napoleon Mill'. Giving it this name, he is taking credit for the construction of the mill despite it being the result of the collective work of the animals. It is worth remembering that the original idea for the windmill was Snowball's, who envisaged a windmill to improve the quality of the animals' lives; this heightens the contrast when we see that Napoleon exploits the windmill for self-aggrandisement. He therefore uses his name to violate the principles of Animalism. Later in the same chapter when Frederick blows up the windmill in the Battle of the Windmill, this action symbolises the death of Animalism. Orwell is making the point that Snowball's dream of a society founded on equality is now absolutely impossible.

By chapter 10, we see the completed and operational windmill, but its original symbolism has changed once more. It now symbolises trade relationships between the animals and the humans: instead of generating electricity for the animals as was originally intended, it is now used to mill corn and generate profits for the pigs. At this point in the novella, the reader is shown how the ideology of Animalism cannot work in practice because, like communist ideology, it does not consider human (or animal) ambition and greed.

Nevertheless, the success of the windmill also comes to represent the ironic triumph of a totalitarian regime in which the pigs now have complete power: it represents the pigs' betrayal of the animals whose lives they had originally wanted to better.

STRUCTURE

FREYTAG'S PYRAMID

Gustav Freytag was a nineteenth-century German novelist, who recognised common patterns in the plots of plays and stories and then developed a diagram to analyse them. The structure of *Animal Farm* can be analysed using this pyramid; interestingly, it can be analysed in two ways.

1: THE CLIMAX IS THE NAPOLEON'S CHOICE TO SEIZE POWER IN CHAPTER 5

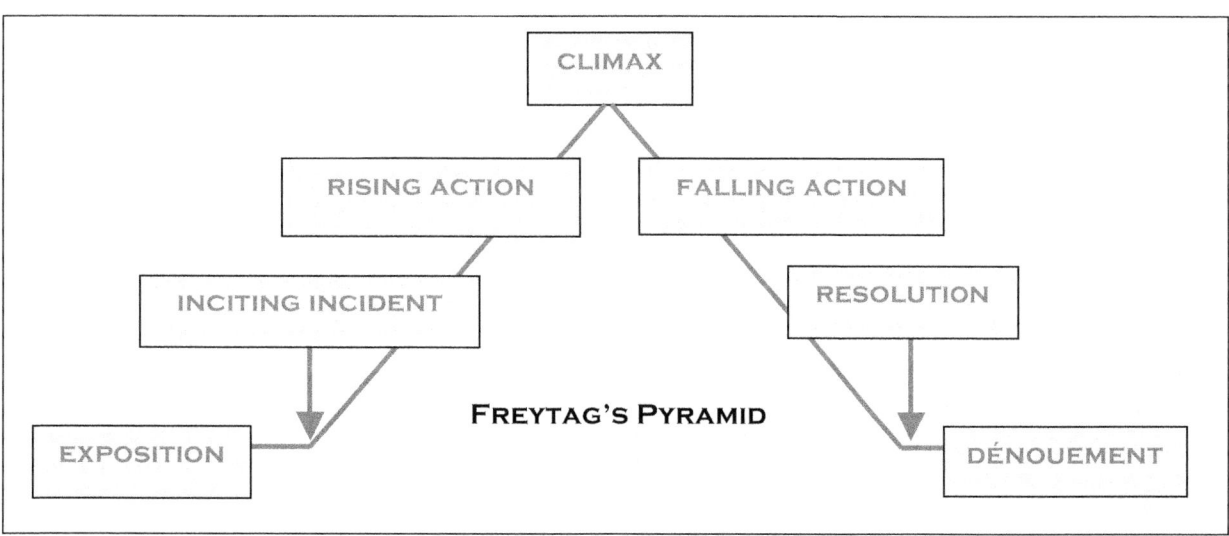

Exposition: the first part of a plot, in which the audience learns about the characters and setting. In chapters 1 and 2, we meet the main characters (the human Mr Jones and the animals, including Napoleon, Snowball, Squealer, Major, and Boxer). We are introduced to the setting of the farm. We learn the animals' thoughts and feelings, particularly in response to old Major's philosophy of Animalism.

Inciting incident (sometimes called complication): something happens to begin the action or conflict. In chapter 2, the drunken Mr Jones forgets to feed the animals, which triggers the rebellion.

Rising action: the story becomes more exciting as conflicts build. The rebellion is successful, and the animals drive the humans off the farm. The animals establish a new society based on the principles of Animalism. The pigs, being the most intelligent animals, take charge. Excitement builds with the Battle of the Cowshed. It builds still further with Napoleon and Snowball's quarrel about the windmill (chapters 2-5).

Climax: the point of greatest tension in a play. The main character comes face-to-face with the conflict and often needs to make a choice. In chapter 5, Napoleon chooses to set his dogs on Snowball, who now flees the farm.

Falling action: the aftermath of the climax. In this case, the aftermath is the consequences of Napoleon's leadership as he asserts his power and consolidates his position, ably assisted by Squealer's propaganda. Napoleon instructs the animals to build the windmill, so their workload increases, and they have less food. Napoleon forges trade alliances with other farmers. He moves to the farmhouse. He spreads propaganda against Snowball when the windmill is destroyed in a storm; he starves the hens to death; forces confessions and orders executions. Under Napoleon's orders, Minimus teaches the animals a song to replace the banned 'Beasts of England'. The animals are encouraged to view Napoleon as a cult figure through Minimus's poem.

Napoleon's trade agreement with Frederick results in the Battle of the Windmill and its subsequent rebuild. The pigs become fatter at the expense of the hungry animals. Animal Farm is proclaimed a Republic and Napoleon its President. Napoleon is now effectively a dictator. Moses returns to the farm, and his religious message makes life under the dictatorship more bearable for some. Napoleon orders the retirement land to be ploughed and used for crops, so the dying and now useless Boxer is taken away by the knacker (chapters 5-9).

Resolution: the main problem or conflict is settled. At the end of chapter 9, the animals believe everything that they are told. The pigs' power is absolute.

Dénouement: the fallout in which any leftover questions, mysteries or secrets are solved. In the final chapter, we see that not one of the original Seven Commandments remains. Hardly anyone remembers life from before the rebellion, and the pigs now have the same status as humans. The animals are still slaves, just as they were before the rebellion. They are in fact worse off because, blinded by propaganda, it does not occur to them to question those in authority.

2: THE CLIMAX IS BOXER'S DEATH IN CHAPTER 9

Exposition: same as above.

Inciting incident: same as above.

Rising action:

- The animals drive the humans off the farm.
- The animals establish a new society and take charge.
- The Battle of the Cowshed.
- Napoleon and Snowball's quarrel about the windmill (chapters 2-5).
- Napoleon sets his dogs on Snowball, who now flees the farm.
- Napoleon instructs the animals to build the windmill, so their workload increases, and they have less food.
- Napoleon forges trade alliances with other farmers.
- Napoleon moves to the farmhouse.
- Napoleon spreads propaganda against Snowball when the windmill is destroyed in a storm.
- Napoleon starves the hens to death.
- Napoleon forces confessions and orders executions.
- Under Napoleon's orders, Minimus teaches the animals a song to replace the banned 'Beasts of England'.
- The animals are encouraged to view Napoleon as a cult figure through Minimus's poem.
- The consequences of Napoleon's trade agreement with Frederick results in the Battle of the Windmill, the windmill's destruction and subsequent rebuild.
- The pigs become fatter at the expense of the hungry animals.
- Animal Farm is proclaimed a republic and Napoleon its president.

- Moses returns to the farm and his religious message makes life under the dictatorship more bearable for the animals.
- Napoleon orders the retirement land to be ploughed and used for crops.

Climax: The ageing and dying Boxer is taken away by the knacker.

Falling action: None.

Resolution: At the end of chapter 9, the animals believe everything that they are told, and the pigs' power is absolute.

Dénouement: See above.

So which analysis by Freytag's Pyramid should we use? There appears to be a strong case for both. The key question to consider when analysing the structure of the novella is *What is the novella about?* Is it about Napoleon's (Stalin's) rise to power or is it about the fate of Boxer, who represents the exploited workers of the regime? Orwell attacks the Soviet regime by highlighting its hypocrisy—so Boxer's death as the climax would help to focus the reader on the plight of the Soviet workers and the failure of communist ideology. However, he also wanted to explore how it was possible for such a regime to gain power—if this was his primary aim, Napoleon driving Snowball away would better fit this purpose. The falling action (which includes Boxer's death) would subsequently serve to focus the attention of the reader on the consequences of Napoleon's absolute power. The reader is therefore invited to consider the nature of a society that allows dictators to rise to power.

CHRONOLOGICAL STRUCTURE

The story is told chronologically, with a gap of an unspecified number of years between the end of chapter 9 and the beginning of chapter 10. At the end of the resolution in chapter 9, the pigs' power is absolute. Orwell's manipulation of time in chapter 10 allows the reader to see how, years later, the pigs have consolidated their power. This puts the reader in a better position to critically evaluate and compare the rise of Animalism to communism.

The fact that by chapter 10 much time has passed makes explicit to the reader how little understanding the animals have of their own history. It is at this point that the reader fully appreciates the power of propaganda to brainwash the animals. The only exception is Benjamin, who cynically states that things never change; ironically, this heightens the tragedy because he could have chosen to involve himself and challenge those in power.

CYCLICAL STRUCTURE

As well as being chronological, the novella might be considered cyclical because, in a sense, it begins where it ends: with a drunken, irresponsible ruler who lives in the farmhouse. To leave no doubt in the reader's mind about Orwell's intentions, the watching animals cannot distinguish the pigs from the humans. Orwell illustrated in this final action his complete cynicism about totalitarianism. He was disillusioned by communist ideology, having seen in Spain that it does not and seemingly cannot work in practice: communism, he believed, could not work and did not improve life for the poor. This is because it failed to consider the all too human greed for power. Interestingly, recent historians have debated the fact that communist leaders like Stalin were in fact 'Red Tsars'.

FORESHADOWING

Orwell employs the structural device of foreshadowing to create a sense of inevitability that the communist regime is doomed to fail. Old Major states 'the life of an animal is misery and slavery', and this foreshadows and prepares us for the conditions the animals later endure after the revolution. Likewise, he states 'Man is the only creature that consumes without producing', which foreshadows the pigs stealing the 'milk and apples', culminating in their luxurious lifestyles when they sleep in the farmhouse on beds, wear clothes and lead a life of privilege. Old Major's reference to the knacker in his speech foreshadows Boxer being taken away by the knacker Alfred Simmons in chapter 9. There are many other examples of foreshadowing in the novella. By using this device, Orwell encourages the reader to reflect upon the political process of apparent change; he invites the reader to consider that communism as a political theory does not work.

LANGUAGE

SIMPLICITY

The language of *Animal Farm* is plain and powerful—and this style of writing reminds us that Orwell was also a journalist. Simple, bare of ornament or rhetorical flourish, Orwell's direct and powerful style is designed to communicate with as many people as possible. This means that readers are better able to access the underlying themes.

There is very little figurative language, but what is there is used to good effect. For example, Old Major employs metaphor when he states that man is the 'root cause of hunger and overwork'. The root imagery focuses the attention of the listeners on the nouns 'hunger and overwork' to demonise humans and to make the point that without humans the animals would live a better lifestyle. The irony is that Old Major naively fails to understand that animals are also capable of oppressing others. Animalism (or communism) ideology is therefore based on flawed assumptions about animal/human nature. This point is developed when Orwell introduces chapter 6 with the simile 'like slaves' to describe how hard the animals work. This develops the irony of them believing that they are free and working for themselves when the reality is they have no freedom at all because their lives are controlled by the pigs.

IRONY

The whole message of *Animal Farm* is ironic because Orwell aims to show that the revolution that seeks to promote equality instead creates another totalitarian society.

Orwell employs three different types of irony:

VERBAL IRONY

Verbal irony is the difference between what a person says and what the person means. It is like sarcasm, the main difference being that with sarcasm the speaker intends to hurt the listener's feelings. With verbal irony, people sometimes say the opposite of what they mean to emphasise a point or to create humour.

Good starting points for exploring verbal irony within the novella are Squealer's speeches. For example, in chapter 5, he tells the animals that Napoleon believes that 'all animals are equal' when explaining why the weekly debates have stopped, positioning Napoleon as better qualified to make decisions than the animals. We therefore have verbal irony because the debates represent an important part of the democratic process: it should not matter if Napoleon agrees with the outcome because the whole point of democracy is that the majority decision rules. By eliminating an essential forum for democratic debates, it is clear to the reader that Napoleon is acting in his own interests—not the interests of the animals. Snowball's use of verbal irony therefore pretends to support the interests of the animals but, defends Napoleon's emerging dictatorship. This is verbal irony in practice.

Situational Irony

To understand situational irony, it is important to understand the context—the situation that the characters are in.

For example, immediately after Old Major tells the animals 'All animals are comrades', the dogs attempt to attack the rats. This is situational irony because the context is that they have been told that all animals are equal. This makes the situation—the dogs attacking the weaker rats—ironic. The outcome is the opposite of what we expect.

Dramatic Irony

With dramatic irony, the audience or readers know something that the characters on stage or in a book do not. Orwell's decision to write the story through the eyes of the animals creates dramatic irony. The readers know, for example, that Squealer has changed the commandments, but the animals believe that they have not remembered them correctly. All along, the reader understands that Squealer is making the changes, and Orwell's use of dramatic irony encourages the reader to make comparisons with the Soviet Union's use of propaganda. There is a harrowing use of dramatic irony when Squealer tells the animals that Boxer has been taken to a vet's and buried. The reader knows that he has been taken by the knacker and can deduce from the crate of whisky that is delivered that the pigs have profited from his death. Orwell therefore uses dramatic irony to draw the attention of the reader to the gullibility of the animals—and by default the Soviet working classes—who allowed the regime to come to power.

Humour

We sometimes see humour in *Animal Farm* through Orwell's use of anthropomorphism, which means to give human characteristics to animals. Do not confuse this with personification. The difference between the two is that with anthropomorphism, the animals are doing something human; with personification, the animals seem to be doing something human.

One example of anthropomorphic humour is when Mollie is caught preening with one of Mrs Jones's ribbons in front of the mirror. Another example in the same paragraph is the revelation that the animals are going to bury some 'hams' that they have found in the farmhouse. The humour is created from the unexpectedly human aspects of the situations. Structurally, Orwell employs these moments of humour to lull the reader into a false sense of security, heightening the impact of the serious message to follow. For example, after the humour of Mollie and the hams, we learn about the Seven Commandments, and then the chapter ends with the mysterious disappearance of the milk. This change in mood focuses the attention of the reader on the difference between the theory of Animalism and the reality of how it does not work in practice. The milk episode contrasts with the humorous ribbon episode to illustrate the hypocrisy of the pigs.

At other times, humour is used for satirical purposes. In chapter 7, for example, we have a list of the hens, goose and a sheep who make confessions before they are quickly executed. The last confession, that of two sheep who murder a ram, contains an element of humour. They killed him by 'chasing him round and round a bonfire when he was suffering from a cough'. This action creates a rather odd, slapstick image in the reader's mind, emphasised by the bathos (a sudden switch to something trivial that changes the mood) of 'suffering from a cough'. Although this is humorous, it heightens the contrast with the brutal execution of the two sheep that immediately follows. Orwell therefore uses satire to draw the reader's attention to the act of execution, inviting the reader to consider the truth of these confessions. The cumulative effect of listing the animals that die becomes overwhelming.

MOTIFS

A motif is a recurring symbol—it might be a concept, object, type of character, or a statement. A motif helps to develop the theme or themes of a text.

Animal Farm contains anthems, songs, poems and slogans, which are all used to control the thoughts of the animals.

'BEASTS OF ENGLAND'

At the beginning of the novella, old Major teaches the animals his rousing anthem 'Beasts of England'. The anthem, which aims to enthuse his listeners, is the counterpart of the Soviet Union's national anthem The Internationale. 'Beasts of England', a propaganda tool to manipulate the animals, contains symbolism of man-made tools (such as 'whips') that oppress the animals and will, following the revolution, vanish when the animals are free. The motif of the whips is discussed in more detail below.

The anthem also contains imagery of food and plenty, as the lyrics depict an enticing picture of a utopia in which everyone has enough. The envisaged utopia is enhanced by a range of persuasive devices. There is sibilance with 'fruitful fields', a soft, gentle sound that creates a sense of longing for better days and satisfaction about what is to come. There is listing of all the crops that will grow in abundance, and the phrase 'golden future time' is repeated at the end of the first and last verse to help the animals to concentrate on the goals of the revolution. Interestingly, the adjective 'golden' connotes wealth and prosperity but this is juxtaposed with 'future time', which is rather vague and implies an unspecified point in the future. This suggests that Orwell's opinion that the envisaged utopia is an unachievable dream. Nevertheless, the anthem that not only summarises Major's thoughts and feelings, but also inspires the animals. This will become particularly important when the animals begin to work 'like slaves', as the anthem will take their minds off their suffering. Not all the animals understand the song, but they can all identify with its positive, uniting, rallying feelings. The rousing anthem serves Major's purpose of focusing the animals on the revolution to come.

In chapter 4, we see how the anthem 'Beasts of England' is used by Snowball and Napoleon as a propaganda tool when they send pigeons to teach the anthem to the animals of neighbouring farms. This provocative act introduces the theme of this chapter, which is international relations and the consolidation of power. In Russia's interwar period (1924-1935), Trotsky's goal was global communism, and he worked hard to encourage a 'permanent world revolution' by utilising the so-called *domino effect*. Trotsky (supporting Karl Marx's 'Workers of the World, Unite!' ideology) wanted Russian communism to inspire the workers of other countries to overthrow their leaders and to forge their own communist regimes like one domino falling and toppling others.

'ANIMAL FARM, ANIMAL FARM'

In chapter 7, Minimus writes the propaganda song 'Animal Farm, Animal Farm' to replace 'Beasts of England' because Napoleon is worried that 'Beasts of England' will rouse the animals to another rebellion.

There is situational irony in the new lyrics:

> Animal Farm, Animal Farm,
> Never through me shalt thou come to harm!

The farm is now more important than the animals: the line 'Never through me shalt thou come to harm!' instils a sense of responsibility in them to protect the farm. We have situational irony, however, because the animals' blood has already been shed; the juxtaposition of not coming to harm with the violence in this chapter illustrates the hypocrisy of communism.

'COMRADE NAPOLEON'

The character of Minimus represents propaganda taking over art to control what people think. In chapter 8, he writes a poem entitled 'Comrade Napoleon', which deliberately contains archaic (old-fashioned) language with the line 'Thou watchest over all'. The archaic subject and verb form 'Thou watchest' has Biblical echoes, implying some sort of god is looking after us. This elevates Napoleon above mere animals and suggests that he is like God. The prayer-like quality of the poem therefore aims to encourage the animals to devote themselves to Napoleon and to worship him from afar. Yet we also have humour because the poem calls Napoleon 'Lord of the swill-bucket!', which makes Napoleon look ridiculous. Orwell therefore employs a reverential tone and mixes it with contrasting elevated and everyday language to mock Napoleon and to parody similar anthems. Perhaps Orwell is suggesting that we should examine all rhetoric more closely.

SLOGANS

When Snowball summarises the Seven Commandments for the animals in a single slogan 'Four legs good, two legs bad', it is on the one hand easier to understand; on the other hand, it ignores the facts that birds are two-legged. Slogans are excellent tools for politicians because they are short and memorable, but they often oversimplify the complicated and untidy nature of real life. The slogan also makes the slow-witted animals more vulnerable because they focus on its propaganda message, and their attention is moved away from the Seven Commandments. This enables the pigs to re-shape their rhetoric away from the guiding principles of socialism. Now that the Seven Commandments have been limited to a single slogan, future debates are also limited. The way is cleared therefore for the pigs to implement their own regime.

The slogan is not only used as a propaganda device to control the thoughts of the animals, but also as a tool for totalitarian oppression. This can be seen when Napoleon teaches the sheep to mindlessly chant 'Four legs good, two legs bad!' to drown out objections in meetings and to interrupt Snowball's speeches. Their incessant bleating bombards the animals with words, making it even more difficult for them to think clearly. We then have further ironic development at the end of the novella when the sheep bleat propaganda with their new slogan 'Four legs good, two legs BETTER!'. This newer propaganda slogan underlines both their lack of intelligence and the emptiness of the rhetoric.

Rituals

After Napoleon seizes power, the pigs increase the number of rituals in the life of Animal Farm. These rituals include songs, ceremonies, speeches and parades, all of which aim to brainwash the animals into supporting the new regime.

First, we see that the revolution is celebrated by a ritual surrounding the new flag in chapter 3. Snowball's flag with its 'hoof and horn' symbolises the animals and mirrors the hammer and sickle symbol of the communists (the hammer represents industrial labourers and the curved blade of the sickle represents the agricultural labourers). The weekly ritual of the ceremony with the flag serves to develop the animals' feelings of solidarity and unity.

By chapter 8, we see the cult of Napoleon develop through the manipulation of his public image. Like Stalin, Napoleon develops a cult of personality to make himself appear all-powerful in the eyes of the animals. On the rare occasions he appears in public, he is surrounded by ceremony: Minimus composes poems about him; a gun is fired to celebrate his birthday; and the animals are expected to praise him (like Christians praise God) when good things happen.

Also in chapter 8, we see further rituals introduced after victory in the battle of the Windmill. There are celebrations, the firing of the gun, the congratulatory speeches and Napoleon's creation of the 'Order of the Green Banner'. On the surface, the Order is a symbol of honour for the dead, yet it is ironic because the pigs ordered the animals to fight for the farm and sacrifice their lives. These 'voluntary' sacrifices have made the totalitarian farm stronger because of its victory. The use of the 'Order of the Green Banner' therefore takes advantage of the animals' feelings of patriotism.

In chapter 9, Orwell employs the rhetorical techniques of the rule of three and repetition when we learn that Napoleon orders 'more songs, more speeches, more processions'. The reader can see that the repetition of 'more' combines with the three nouns to create a tone of weariness—the downtrodden animals' free time is being controlled through the pigs' use of ritual. The songs, speeches and processions are therefore used to control the thoughts of the exhausted animals and to indoctrinate them with the values of the totalitarian regime. They define the workers' sense of identity and mould their thoughts.

In the same chapter, Orwell employs more irony with the weekly 'Spontaneous Demonstration' that Napoleon introduces. The adjective 'spontaneous' means to happen as an impulse, without prior thought or planning. We learn that the demonstrations, ordered by Napoleon, are anything but spontaneous. This word play focuses the attention of the reader on the nature of the demonstrations, which the pigs are using to manipulate the feelings of the animals. The adjective 'spontaneous' implies that the demonstrations are part of a meaningless, mechanical process, with the animals being devoid of genuine feelings of happiness and spontaneity. This in turn draws attention to the oppression that the animals are experiencing.

After Boxer dies, Napoleon announces that there will be a commemorative feast and a wreath. On the surface, the wreath is a symbol to commemorate the horse; however, Napoleon uses it to threaten the other animals and to remind them that, like Boxer, they must 'work harder'. Orwell's use of the wreath therefore illustrates the opportunistic and self-serving nature of the pigs, even at a memorial event.

At the beginning and end of the novella, Orwell makes contrasting use of the trappings of ritual. Initially, Napoleon in chapter 5 gives the order for the animals to disinter old Major's skull and place it by the flagstaff and gun. The skull serves as a useful visual aid for the pigs' propaganda, symbolising the Animalism cause. By openly displaying it, Napoleon appears to be aligning himself with Animalism to consolidate his power. This strategy is like Stalin's when in 1924 he ordered Lenin's body to be embalmed and put on public display. In chapter 10, however, we learn about Napoleon's decision to bury the skull. By removing the skull from the sight of the animals, he is removing the ideology it represents and encouraging them to focus on him instead. Similarly, Napoleon removes the 'hoof and horn' symbols of the revolution from the flag so that the animals are discouraged from reflecting too much upon the freedom and self-determination that the revolution promised.

Ribbons

Ribbons are a recurring motif throughout the novella. We first see them associated with Mollie, who represents the selfish and shallow materialism of the Russian middle classes who value their possessions and money. Her preoccupations with 'ribbons' and 'sugar' symbolise vanity and self-indulgence. In chapter 2, Mollie emerges as less enthusiastic about Animalism than many of the other animals; Snowball throws her ribbons into the fire because only humans should wear them. Orwell parodies the superficiality and materialism of the middle and aristocratic classes when Pilkington bribes Mollie with 'ribbons' and 'sugar' to leave Animal Farm. This act represents the decision of many disaffected Russians, called White Russians, to emigrate in the hope of a better life.

These White Russians supported the tsar and emigrated *en masse* from the Soviet Union around the time of the Russian Civil War, from around 1918 to 1921. They were generally dispossessed landowners, factory owners, members of the church, royalists—in short, anyone opposed to the Bolsheviks. As members of the former Russian Empire, they had often received special treatment, such as Mollie receiving 'ribbons' and 'sugar' from Mr Jones. They did not mind serving the tsar, just as Mollie does not mind pulling the cart.

We see the corruption of the socialist idea of equality in chapter 9 when Orwell employs the ribbon motif to emphasise class differences: suddenly, pigs can wear 'green ribbons' on Sundays. Ribbons are therefore used as a motif to illustrate that the pigs have become more and more like the elitist regime they have replaced.

Bowler Hat

The 'bowler hat' symbolises human cruelty. In chapter 8, Napoleon wears the bowler hat that used to belong to Mr Jones, so we immediately see that it is associated with tyranny and exploitation. Napoleon first wears the bowler hat when he finds the whisky and becomes drunk; the bowler hat and whisky, both associated with the hated Mr Jones, emphasise Orwell's point that a new tyrant is replacing the old. A chapter later, we see that the van driver too is wearing a bowler hat. This symbolises that Boxer, being transported against his will to the knacker's yard, is trapped by the power of a totalitarian regime.

Whips

'Whips' symbolise the abuse of power, cruelty and exploitation of others. They are first mentioned in the 'Beasts of England' anthem; this prepares the reader for the horror of seeing Mr Jones whipping the hungry animals in chapter 2.

The symbolism of the whip slightly changes after the animals have driven Jones away from the farm. The animals throw the whips in the fire, signifying their rejection of the tyrannical regime; the destruction of the whips is symbolic of revolution and freedom.

In chapter 9, the van driver has a whip, which he uses fiercely on his horses to speed Boxer away. The whip and bowler hat motifs combine and emphasise the fact that this human—like Mr Jones—will not change, and he has complete power over others.

The completeness of the pigs' transformation is seen in the use of the simple sentence 'He carried a whip in his trotter' to describe Napoleon in Chapter 10. Previously, whips were associated with human tyranny; now, they are associated with the tyranny of the pigs. Both the whip and the bowler hat are motifs that confirm that the new totalitarian regime is no better than the old.

THEME: THE POWER OF LANGUAGE

OLD MAJOR'S SPEECH

Before analysing old Major's speech, it is worth summarising the ideology of Animalism. The central principle is that the 'life of an animal is misery and slavery' and that 'Man is the only creature that consumes without producing'. Old Major, whose character is a combination of Marx and Engels, says 'Remove man from the scene, and the root cause of hunger and overwork is abolished for ever'. This confident assertion echoes the *Communist Manifesto*, which states that, with no ruling class, the populace will collectively own property and resources, so that everyone will have enough: 'From each according to his abilities, to each according to his needs'. Marx, Engels and old Major see the proletariat (i.e. the working classes/the animals) as victims exploited by the capitalist ruling classes, who own the businesses, the factories and the shops. The fruits of the workers' labour on the factory floor etc. are taken from them by the owners, who do no work of their own. The proletariat's labour brings the workers no reward but instead makes the owners rich.

Orwell uses the adjective 'old' five times in the first two chapters when referring to Major. The word 'old' emphasises not only his age and impending death, which engages the sympathy of his listeners, but also reinforces the fact that his wisdom is the result of a lifetime of thinking. The anecdote about his reflections over the years adds further impact, as anecdotes are an effective device to capture the attention of an audience. Interestingly, his name Major is the opposite of *minor*, indicating Marx's great influence in spreading the communist message and changing the lives of millions of people.

Major's speech in chapter 1 is full of persuasive rhetorical devices to win the animals over to his ideology of 'Animalism'. For example, his first word to them is 'Comrades'. By employing this inclusive term of address, Major aims to unite the animals; he repeats 'comrades' throughout his speech to encourage these feelings of animal togetherness. In the Soviet Union, 'comrades' was a common form of address; it implies a shared life in which everyone is valued, considered equal and a friend. Major uses other inclusive words throughout his speech, such as 'friends' and the pronouns 'you and I' and 'we'. He directly addresses them using 'you'. These techniques aim to make the listeners engage and agree with his thoughts.

Major also employs a range of rhetorical questions as a structural feature of his speech. For example, he asks 'what is the nature of this life of ours?'. Having gained the attention of the animals, he sets them up to think about the question before answering it. The old pig continues to employ rhetorical questions to guide the thought processes of the animals throughout his speech and to make his argument more forceful.

Furthermore, he frequently uses repetition to emphasise his ideas. For example: '-Man. Man is the only real enemy we have. Remove Man from the scene, and the root cause of hunger and overwork is abolished for ever'. The repetition of 'Man' successfully positions humans as the enemy. The strength of old Major's feelings is reinforced by Orwell's capitalisation of 'Man', stereotyping human beings, elevating them to an almost demonic status. It is interesting that Major does not personalise Mr and Mrs Jones by using their names; using the noun 'Man' depersonalises the targets of the rebellion and makes it easier for his listeners to engage with his ideas. This is further reinforced with the use of consonance with 'Remove Man' as he calls the animals to action. The metaphor of humans being the 'root cause' of all the problems is effective, as it relates to agriculture, and his listeners on the farm understand that roots grow and flourish as part of a chain of events. The rural imagery and the equation of 'Man' as the 'root cause' makes the solution to their problem of 'hunger and overwork' (note how emotive and empathetic these words are) simple to identify. Furthermore, the inclusive 'we' and the imperative 'Remove Man from the scene' aims to rouse them to action.

Old Major also employs contrasting ideas to emphasise his points. For example, he states 'Man is the only creature that consumes without producing'. The contrasts of 'consumes' and 'without producing' are further heightened by the hissing sibilance ('consumes' – 'producing') and double assonance ('consumes' – 'producing'). These devices focus the attention of the listener on the class differences and help to build momentum. The alliteration with 'creature' and 'consumes' further dehumanises people, who are described as animals rather than human beings. Interestingly, the verb 'consume' means to eat, drink or purchase. It is also quite an unemotional word, suggesting that humans unthinkingly and perhaps automatically take everything from the animals. Orwell's contrasts between animal and man, reinforced by sound patterns, symbolise the tensions between the classes in the pre-revolutionary Russian Empire.

The momentum develops through a range of well-chosen rhetorical devices. Talking about 'Man', old Major states: 'He does not give milk, he does not lay eggs' before listing more things that Mr Jones is unable to do. The repetition and parallelism of the clauses adds rhythm and weight to his words, making them easier for his listeners to understand and remember. Carefully manipulating sentence length, Major contrasts the long list describing the laziness of 'Man' with a short sentence for emphasis: 'Yet he is lord of all the animals'. The assonance with 'lord of all' emphasises the difference in social status and reminds us of the Russian feudal system. By calling Mr Jones a 'lord', Major is heightening the contrast between 'Man' and animals. The phrase 'lord of all' also reminds us inevitably of God, perhaps implying there will be no place for God in the post-revolution society. This is further emphasised by the absence of Moses, the only creature not present at the meeting. This phrase 'lord of all' might also foreshadow that Napoleon will become lord of all animals—as Minimus reverentially says in his 'Comrade Napoleon' poem, 'Lord of the swill-bucket!'.

Old Major's powerful imagery adds impact to his speech—for example, the personification of the 'cruel knife' that pursues the animals to the slaughter. This is a horrific image which emphasises how the animals are the oppressed victims of Mr Jones's totalitarian regime. There is the vivid and emotive use of 'scream' to recreate the 'horror' of slaughter when the animals (which he lists for impact) will 'scream' their last breath. The use of the word 'scream' heightens the emotional impact and terror of his words.

Another interesting device is old Major's use of slogans. For example, he says 'All men are enemies. All animals are comrades'. Slogans are excellent tools for politicians because they are short and memorable. Some of the animals are not particularly clever, so the grammatical parallelism is a good memory aid. The antithesis with 'men' and 'animals' followed by 'enemies' and 'comrades' emphasises his point, heightening the differences and developing the animals' sense of injustice.

Old Major's speech is significant because he makes it clear to the animals that they have the power to change their lives. He envisages a utopia in which 'all animals are equal', achieved through 'rebellion!'. Like Marx and Engels, old Major criticises the totalitarian rule of Mr Jones and incites revolution; he fails, however, to provide detail about the management of his utopian dream. This might suggest that he is a dreamer rather than a realist.

Orwell symbolises the potentially totalitarian nature of communism by the placement of animals in the barn. When Major delivers his speech, he speaks from a 'raised platform', echoing his higher status, while the dogs and pigs position themselves in 'front' of him, also suggesting a higher status because they are closer to the leader. Orwell employs this symbolism to suggest that while the principles of socialism or communism (Marx and Engels used these terms interchangeably) do consider human nature, they fail to re-educate human nature. Orwell's use of the 'raised platform' suggests that there will always be a Stalin or a Lenin who will hijack the ideal society and pervert it to his own end, thereby corrupting socialist ideas.

As the novella unfolds, the reader will appreciate the growing irony in old Major's speech and anthem. His assertion that 'All animals are comrades' will prove to be untrue. Furthermore, he states that the animals must not become like men after the revolution. Of course, at the end of the novella, we will see the pigs develop a hierarchical regime that results in them becoming indistinguishable from humans—and, even worse, the animals are living in a totalitarian state so without any freedom of speech. Old Major means well, but he is naïve about the nature of animals. In turn, the animals are blinded by his rhetoric and do not understand the difference between a utopian dream and the reality of life.

SQUEALER

Squealer is defined by his persuasive ability as an orator. His very name clearly invokes the squealing of pigs: the onomatopoeic verb *squeal* refers to an unpleasant, shrill sound, suggesting that his propaganda, however unwelcome to the ears, demands to be heard. Informally, *squeal* can mean to protest or complain. Squealer vigorously defends Napoleon's decisions, protesting any dissent from the animals. Another informal meaning of *squeal* is to inform against someone. This connotes the communist regime, which brewed mistrust, thereby foreshadowing future confessions and executions. Squealer also betrays the animals and the ideology of Animalism with his propaganda.

Squealer speaks on behalf of Napoleon for the first time in chapter 2; his historical counterpart is Molotov, Stalin's head of communist propaganda. Squealer might also represent the Soviet newspaper *Pravda*, which was used by Stalin for indoctrination purposes.

Orwell employs the clause 'skipping from side to side' to describe Squealer's movements when he is speaking to the animals. This literally describes his movements but metaphorically illustrates how he skips around points with his arguments. The rapid movement of the skipping connotes a quick-thinking mind; skipping is also a game, implying that Squealer enjoys the mind games he plays with his propaganda, suggesting a lack of empathy for the other animals. Furthermore, the skipping movement implies a shifting of the ground, a lack of certainty or solidity or even truth, so Orwell invites the reader to mistrust his words.

We first see the importance of Squealer's propaganda in justifying to the animals that it is necessary for the pigs to have the 'milk and apples'; his words are positioned at the end of chapter 3 for maximum impact. He confuses the animals with pseudo-science, and he lies to persuade them that the benefits of 'milk and apples' are essential to the pigs, the so-called 'brainworkers', who are ceaselessly striving for the common good of the animals. Through the character of Squealer, the reader becomes aware that the 'All animals are equal' ideology is breaking down and that the pigs are raising themselves to a privileged class.

His lack of conscience can be seen in chapter 3 and elsewhere in the novella when he employs a scare tactic to persuade the animals to his point of view. Squealer invokes the idea of Mr Jones returning, reinforcing it with the repetition of the exclamatory sentence: 'Jones would come back!' This heightens the psychological impact of his words because threatening the animals with the names of their enemies is an effective strategy to scare the simpler animals and thereby maintain power. Squealer often pretends to side with the animals and persuade them that he is acting for the common good when the reality is that he is speaking on behalf of Napoleon. By invoking the names of Jones (and later, Snowball), Squealer and Napoleon are suggesting that they are the only true saviours of the farm and its inhabitants. This scare tactic also aims to convince the animals that their life is better now than under the previous regime.

In chapter 5, Squealer uses more strategies to manipulate the animals. He deliberately confuses them with jargon, such as the word 'tactics', which he repeats to mystify them. In a similar way to his 'milk and apples' propaganda, he positions Napoleon as a martyr who is sacrificing his own desires to help the animals, pretending that leadership is not something he enjoys. Another strategy that he uses is to rewrite history by telling the animals that Snowball's heroics in the Battle of the Cowshed were 'much exaggerated'. He develops this strategy later in the chapter when he tells the animals that the idea for the windmill had really been Napoleon's all along and not Snowball's. All these strategies position Napoleon in a positive light.

Another tactic that Squealer uses is to deliberately baffle the animals, either through words or statistics. For example, in chapter 6, he manipulates language to define what a bed is in order to confuse the animals and to stop them from questioning the pigs' decision to sleep in beds. In chapter 8, he employs false statistics to manipulate the thoughts of the animals. Benjamin Disraeli, twice Prime Minister of England, is believed to have said 'There are three kinds of lies: Lies, damned lies, and statistics'. Squealer reads lists of numbers to the exhausted animals, statistics that aim to prove their lives are better than before. The uneducated, unintelligent animals are too tired to challenge his claims. Despite the contrary evidence of hunger all around, Squealer's lies and statistics convince the animals that they must be wrong.

An important element of Squealer's propaganda role is to rewrite history. When Orwell was a resistance fighter in Spain, he noticed that some newspapers inaccurately reported historical events such as battles or chose not to report them at all (this is reflected in Winston Smith's job at the ironically named Ministry of Truth in Orwell's final novel, *Nineteen Eighty-Four*). Squealer distorts historical facts in chapter 6 when he says that the animals must have dreamed the resolution banning money and trade beyond the farm. To reinforce the point, Napoleon's dogs create a threatening presence by growling at the four disbelieving young pigs. It is clear to the reader at this point in the novella that the use of threat to support propaganda is an effective persuasive tool. This heightens the contrast with earlier in the novella when the animals and Snowball might have debated the issue of forging trade links with other farms.

In Russia, Stalinists also distorted historical facts to suit their purposes. Evidence of this can be seen by googling: *Soviet censorship of images during Stalin's regime*. The photographs provide evidence that Stalin's regime altered them by removing images of people who fell out of favour. This distortion of history is seen in the novella when Squealer announces in chapter 7 that, despite appearances, Snowball was in 'league with Jones', even when apparently fighting for the animals at the Battle of the Cowshed. The bemused animals slowly accept the pigs' version of history despite some of them having taken part in the battle. Napoleon has rewritten the past to turn Snowball from hero to villain, to use him as a convenient scapegoat to explain anything and everything that goes wrong on the farm. The pigs have therefore completely rewritten history to focus the attention of the animals outwards on a common enemy and to develop a sense of national pride so that they do not criticise the current regime. By rewriting the past, the pigs manipulate the present and control the thoughts of the animals, who are unable to see through the lies.

Perhaps the most significant act of porcine propaganda is the series of alterations made to the Seven Commandments, alterations which justify more privileges for the pigs. The reader assumes that Squealer (under the direction of Napoleon) is responsible for the rewriting because at the end of chapter 8, he is found unconscious at the foot of the commandments next to a broken ladder, a lamp, a paintbrush and a tin of paint. In chapter 6, it is clear that the pigs are manipulating language to increase their status and the benefits that come with a higher position in society. For example, the commandment 'No animal shall sleep in a bed' changes to 'No animal shall sleep in a bed with sheets'. This is, of course, contrary to the principles of Animalism: the pigs are literally rewriting history. Stalin and other high-ranking members of the communist party came to enjoy privileges like those of the tsar, so Orwell's use of the Seven Commandments alerts the reader to the fact that tyranny is cyclical: one tyrant replaces another.

Orwell also employs satire to reveal the faults in Squealer's propaganda. For example, after the Battle of the Windmill in chapter 8, Squealer employs false logic to convince the animals that they were victorious, despite their heavy losses and injuries. Squealer explains to them that it is a victory because they have won back the farm; however, the injured Boxer replies 'Then we have won back what we had before'. Without understanding what he has done, Boxer has made clear to the animals and the readers the emptiness of Squealer's propaganda.

In chapter 9, we see how Squealer carefully employs words with particular connotations to influence the thoughts of the animals. For example, he uses the noun 'readjustment' when he explains that he is cutting the animals' rations. To readjust means to adapt something, and it is a euphemism (a mild way of saying something unpleasant). The differences in connotations are subtle but effective: readjusting something creates a less daunting mental image in the minds of the animals. It means that they are more likely to accept the cuts, perceiving them instead as less threatening changes.

In the same chapter, there is further manipulation of language when Animal Farm is announced as a 'Republic'. A republic is a state in which the people have the power, and they are led by an elected president. The use of the word 'republic' therefore suggests that the principles of Animalism are being maintained. Of course, the reality is completely different, especially when we learn that Napoleon is 'elected' President. The verb 'elected' is used ironically because it is obvious to the reader that he is already in power and has simply changed his title and the name of the state. It is also news to the animals, illustrating that they have not been involved in the so-called democratic process. Manipulating language in this way effectively hoodwinks the gullible animals into believing that they have more power than they actually have and that they are better off than they were before.

Finally, Orwell illustrates the power of Squealer's language by the animals' response to it: they appear to be unable or unwilling to see that they are being lied to. For example, in chapter 9, they believe Squealer when he tells them about the expensive and admirable care that the dying Boxer received. Orwell says that the animals are relieved to hear that Boxer received every attention: they want to believe in Napoleon, choosing to ignore the evidence written on the side of the knacker's van that the horse's ultimate destination is a glue factory. Perhaps they choose to believe Squealer's lies because the alternative, the reality of Boxer's death, would mean that the animals must examine their consciences. Life is much easier if you conform and do not take the risk of challenging the regime.

Minimus

Minimus becomes a more prominent character from chapter 7, and his function illustrates how communist propaganda influenced art in the Soviet Union. Lenin understood the importance of propaganda in the production of art. He stated: 'Every artist, everyone who considers himself an artist, has the right to create freely according to his ideal, independently of everything. However, we are communists and we must not stand with folded hands and let chaos develop as it pleases. We must systemically guide this process and form its result.'

From the 1930s, Stalin set up organisations that composers (as well as writers and artists) had to join if they wanted to be performed or published. Their art had to reflect Social Realism, the celebration and glorification of communist values, using realistic imagery. Government committees firmly controlled all creative output, and artists had to submit their work for approval. Composers produced pro-Stalinist pieces and nationalist songs, often based on traditional folk melodies.

The quality of Minimus's government-controlled output is discussed above in the **Language** chapter under the *Motif* subheadings of *'Animal Farm, Animal Farm'* and *'Comrade Napoleon'*. Orwell deliberately satirises the output of Minimus to mock state-sponsored art and rhetoric and to show the hypocrisy of communism.

Moses and Religion

Moses represents the Russian Orthodox Church. The name Moses reminds us of the biblical Moses, who led his people out of Egypt into the Promised Land. Moses the raven in the novella represents religion's role as offering hope to the animals.

Moses makes their hard lives on the farm easier to endure when he promises that after death all animals will go to 'Sugarcandy Mountain', which symbolises heaven. In American folk songs dating back to the 19th century, there is a well-known tradition of the Big Rock Candy Mountain—a sort of heaven on earth. Orwell may have borrowed and repurposed this Americanism. Closer to England, we must remember that from 1940, sugar was rationed, so its status as a luxury item in World War II was more pronounced at the time that Orwell wrote the novella. The reference to 'Sugarcandy Mountain' would probably be quite mouth-watering to the sugar-deprived post-war reader (rationing of sweets and sugar was finally lifted in 1953) and 'Mountain' evokes thoughts of abundance.

Mr Jones uses Moses' descriptions of Sugarcandy Mountain to manipulate the animals, to give them promises about a paradisal afterlife whilst cruelly exploiting them in the present. In chapter 2, we learn that Moses is the Joneses' favourite pet. Mr Jones feeds him 'bread soaked in beer', which reminds us of the bread and wine used in communion, symbolising the affinity in this case between church and state (i.e. Moses and Mr Jones). This act also symbolises the tsar manipulating the church elders through bribes; in return, the church controlled the working classes by telling the illiterate population that God decided who was tsar, so challenging the tsar was like challenging God. They should therefore accept life as it was because it was the will of God; this aimed to dissuade the poor from challenging those in power.

In the Russian Empire, the sympathy and support between the monarchy and the Church was clearly a threat to the communist movement. After the revolution, the Bolsheviks needed to isolate and destroy the powerful Russian church with its millions of supporters; this is mirrored in *Animal Farm* when we learn that the pigs must 'argue very hard' to counteract the raven's story about 'Sugarcandy Mountain'. The pigs counter Moses' promises of Sugarcandy Mountain by calling them 'lies'. In the Soviet Union, the communists discouraged public worship, positioning science against what they called religious superstition. The Bolsheviks justified this by quoting Karl Marx, who in 1844 wrote: 'Religion is the sigh of the oppressed creature, the heart of a heartless world, and the soul of soulless conditions. It is the opium of the people'. In other words, according to the Bolsheviks, religion ('lies') is like a drug that creates pleasant, calming illusions. As a result, the proletariat or working classes do not have the energy or will to challenge their capitalist oppressors, who continue to exploit them. Interestingly, Marx's views on religion were more positive. He regarded it as a sensible solution to a problem— like taking a painkiller for a painful condition, religion is 'like a drug that creates pleasant, calming illusions'. This is a much more positive interpretation. Marx also regarded religion as a solution generated by the people rather than imposed on them from above. This is an interesting point in *Animal Farm* because Mr Jones does not impose the idea of Sugarcandy Mountain; it comes from Moses, who is initially supported by the animals.

Moses' disappearance from the farm symbolises the separation of church and state in November 1917. To make the act of worship as difficult as possible, the Communist Party executed and imprisoned hundreds of priests, destroyed many churches and expropriated (took for themselves) church property. Lenin's persecution of the Russian Orthodox Church successfully eliminated its threat to the Communist Party's power.

The reader begins to appreciate the cyclical nature of tyranny when Moses returns in chapter 9. Just as Mr Jones gave him 'bread soaked in beer', the pigs give him an allowance of 'beer' every day and allow him to stay on the farm despite telling the animals that his stories are 'lies'. This parallels the communists allowing the return of the Russian Orthodox Church after World War II. Both the pigs and the communists came to understand that the workers needed the hope (or delusion) of a better future to endure their current lives, thereby reducing the likelihood of another rebellion. 'Sugarcandy Mountain' had always provided hope for that better future. We therefore see that the pigs use religion to control society in the same way as Mr Jones or the tsar.

THEME: REVOLUTION

THE KEY PLAYERS

In ***Animal Farm* and Historical Parallels,** chapter 1, we compared old Major's speech with the *Communist Manifesto*. His speech is also analysed in detail in the chapter entitled **Theme: The Power of Language**.

In chapter 2, the revolution happens very quickly, and it is interesting to note that Orwell describes the 'animals' that take part as a collective group, rather than individually by name, symbolising their equality and echoing the communist ideology of the unity of workers.

In the same chapter, we learn that old Major dies before he sees the revolution; Karl Marx also died (34 years) before the Russian Revolution, which took place nearly 70 years after the *Communist Manifesto* was published. After Lenin's death, Trotsky and Stalin competed for power. Similarly, Snowball and Napoleon are rivals for power after Old Major's death. From this point onwards, the animals attempt to live by the tenets of communism, and the reader sees the widening gulf between communism in theory and communism in practice.

As a group, the pigs represent the intelligentsia who masterminded the Russian Revolution. Classical or orthodox Marxism assumes that after a revolution, there will be an intermediate state—'the dictatorship of the proletariat'—which will, amongst other things, suppress any attempted bourgeois counter-revolution. Lenin infamously believed in 'diversity in discussion but unity in action'. The fact that the proletariat would have to act with force and determination to neutralise opposition at any and every stage was never doubted. Stalin followed this with his own version of the dictatorship of the proletariat, ruthlessly eliminating not only the bourgeois but also other ostensibly Marxist-Leninist rivals to his position. This is a paradox that Orwell explores as his central theme in *Animal Farm* when the pigs become human.

Orwell's choice of names for the pigs suggests their personalities and roles in the revolution. Old Major and Squealer have already been discussed, so we will explore the significance of the names of Napoleon and Snowball.

NAPOLEON

Based on the historical figure of Stalin, Napoleon the pig is, we assume, named after Napoleon Bonaparte, who rose to prominence in the French Revolution. The French regarded him as a liberator until he crowned himself emperor two years after the 1802 French Revolutionary Wars. He then restored the aristocracy, handing titles to close friends and family, just as Napoleon eliminated Mr Jones and his family and workers, then replaced them with his fellow pigs.

In terms of personality traits, Napoleon Bonaparte was a strong and ambitious leader. Napoleon the pig looks 'fierce', and possesses an aggressive, dominant and intimidating personality. These character traits become more apparent as the novella unfolds until by the end, he is indistinguishable from the visiting farmers.

SNOWBALL

As a verb, *to snowball* means to increase or to expand or spread quickly; Snowball's name might be a metaphor for his desire for the communist ideology to snowball to other countries. Trotsky, like Marx and Engels, wanted world communism (a permanent revolution). Snowball's desire to spread communist ideology to other farms is made clear when he sends pigeons to neighbouring farms to teach other animals 'Beasts of England'.

Snowball is 'more vivacious' than Napoleon, 'quicker in speech and more inventive'. The pointed comparison between the two pigs reveals Snowball's superior appeal and even charisma. When Snowball initiates the building of the windmill, we see that he is a progressive politician. His main historical counterpart is Trotsky, but he also contains elements of Lenin—Lenin was a clever and faithful interpreter of Marxism, and Snowball is a clever and faithful interpreter of Animalism. As

Snowball's plans for the windmill grow, so will his troubles snowball in the face of Napoleon's opposition.

Snowball, like Trotsky, sets up committees; this clearly illustrates his support for the ideology of Animalism. We learn, however, that he is politically naïve and idealistic as these projects fail. For example, the 'Wild Comrade's Re-education Committee' is a paradox in itself: a wild animal cannot change its nature. We therefore see that Snowball is like old Major in that, despite their intellect and noble ideas, they are both naïve and unable to understand animal nature; the failed committees symbolise the failure of Animalism.

Snowball's name has resonance throughout the novella on other levels. After the death of Lenin, Trotsky and Stalin competed for power; these struggles increase between Snowball and Napoleon until Snowball is chased off the farm. Later in the novella, Napoleon employs propaganda against Snowball, and the fear of Snowball snowballs: he is painted as an increasingly evil if ghostly presence, which symbolises the communists demonising Trotsky.

POWER STRUGGLES

The worsening relationship between Napoleon and Snowball is mirrored in the pathetic fallacy of the 'bitterly hard' January weather at the beginning of chapter 5. These words reflect the nature of their debates: on the surface, the pigs appear to be simply debating policy. In reality, they are competing for power, and these debates mirror the increasing power struggles between Stalin and Trotsky, particularly after Lenin's death. The two pigs are at loggerheads just as their two historical antecedents were in deathly rivalry with each other, and this heightens the differences between them.

We see the sharpest differences between Napoleon and Snowball in their attitudes towards the windmill. At this point in the novella (the symbolism changes later), the windmill represents technical progress and modernisation. Snowball sees it as a means for the farm to become more self-sufficient. Like Trotsky, Snowball is an intellectual and a planner, who thinks long-term and considers the future of the animals. He focuses on using the windmill for the good of the animals in line with the principles of Animalism. By way of contrast, Napoleon wants the animals to have little or no leisure because, if they are working hard, they will not have any free time to think about their hard lives and they will be easier for him to control. Rather than winning Snowball around through discussion, Napoleon contemptuously urinates on his carefully drawn plans. Napoleon thinks only of the present because he wants to establish himself as a totalitarian ruler. It becomes increasingly apparent that, as a concept, the windmill is as difficult for Snowball and all the other animals to attain as Sugarcandy Mountain.

Another contrast between the pigs is in their persuasive techniques. Just as Trotsky was a superb orator, so Snowball wins the animals to his point of view with his 'brilliant speeches'. He wins people over through logic and rhetoric, which contrasts with Napoleon, who is not interested in debate and freedom of speech. In fact, as Squealer says, Napoleon employs 'tactics' to control the animals by packing the barn with sheep, which he has taught to interrupt Snowball's speeches by saying 'Four legs good, two legs bad'. Orwell paints such sharp contrasts between the clever and charismatic Snowball and the sinister and secretive Napoleon that it is easy to suppose Orwell himself sympathises with Snowball's plight. Perhaps Orwell's experience in the Spanish Civil War (he joined a Trotskyist political group that was persecuted by the communists) influences his depiction of Snowball.

THEME: TYRANNY, THE ABUSE OF POWER AND THE CORRUPTION OF ANIMALISM

We have seen that Orwell chose to write an allegory as a vehicle to criticise totalitarianism; because of Orwell's experiences in Spain, we also know that he hated any political system that allowed itself to be corrupted by totalitarian tendencies.

This broadens the meaning of the allegory, as it is no longer solely about the Soviet Union: it can be interpreted on a symbolic level to cover all kinds of totalitarian regimes. Orwell aimed to expose the corruption behind these regimes.

MR AND MRS JONES

The first tyrannical regime that we encounter is that of Mr Jones, who represents Tsar Nicholas II. He and Mrs Jones hold positions at the top of a strictly hierarchical society, over which he has complete power.

We are introduced to the theme of tyranny and the abuse of power in the first paragraph of chapter 1: the positioning of the theme signifies its importance. Although we see very little of Mr Jones, Orwell places him at the beginning and end of the first chapter to signal the importance of his role as a violent dictator. The animals are placed in the middle of the chapter, symbolising their oppression by Mr Jones. The bulk of the chapter focuses on the interactions between the animals, however, suggesting that they—the proletariat—are of greater importance than the corrupt regime under which they live.

Both Mr and Mrs Jones are portrayed as irresponsible and lazy. In the first paragraph, we learn that Mrs Jones is in bed and Mr Jones is 'too drunk to remember to shut the pop-holes'. A pop-hole is a small opening (for example, in a chicken coop) for animals to pass through; by leaving the pop-holes open, the animals are at risk from foxes. The adjective 'drunk' illustrates the farmer's self-indulgence and irresponsibility. His shocking lack of concern for the well-being of the animals in his care mirrors the irresponsibility of the Tsar. The open pop-holes might also symbolise class divisions breaking down, foreshadowing old Major's Animalism speech. Ironically, the negligent Mr Jones unwittingly allows the animals to pass through the pop-holes and attend old Major's meeting, so his actions facilitate the animals' later rebellion.

Mr Jones provides visual evidence of the self-indulgence that old Major describes in his speech (this also foreshadows the pigs' later behaviour). In the first paragraph of the novella, we learn that he 'lurched' towards the farmhouse, illustrating to the reader that he is drunk. His decision to take another drink to bed emphasises his laziness, gluttony and inability to nurture anyone but himself.

Like a tyrant, Mr Jones employs violence when under threat, and there are many parallels that can be drawn with Nicholas the Bloody, as the tsar was called by his political opponents. At the end of chapter 1, Mr Jones thinks that he is firing his gun at a 'fox in the yard'. Like the tsar, he wants to protect his assets and is prepared to resort to violence to maintain power (such as his response to the 1905 revolution when The Imperial Guard fired upon unarmed demonstrators, killing 200 people and wounding 800 more). The fox is an interesting choice of animal for Orwell to include, as traditionally, foxes are depicted as sly and cunning; the intelligent fox connotes evil and corruption, which might foreshadow the pigs' rise to power. Finally, we see situational irony in the fact that whilst Mr Jones is employing violence to maintain control, he is completely unaware that the animals themselves are planning a revolution.

THE PIGS

After Mr Jones leaves the farm, the pigs gradually change into tyrants who abuse their power.

At first, their transition seems innocuous enough. All new governments need a constitution—a set of agreed principles to govern a state and govern behaviour. In chapter 2, the pigs admit that they have been secretly learning to read and write, and that they have put these skills to good use by painting the 'Seven Commandments' on the barn wall. This very act hints that the pigs aspire to control the other animals because—contrary to the rules of Animalism—the Seven Commandments were agreed by the pigs only, with no consultation of the other animals.

Orwell's use of the phrase 'Seven Commandments' is a direct allusion to the ten commandments in the Bible. We can break these commandments down into specific categories: there are commandments that link to morality such as 'No animal shall kill any other animal'; there are detailed instructions on how not to be like the human oppressors such as 'No animal shall drink alcohol'; and, of course, 'All animals are equal'. These commandments are clearly visible to all the animals, suggesting transparency and a desire for permanent change. The concept of permanence is like the Biblical Ten Commandments, which were engraved on stone tablets. Throughout history, people have broken the Ten Commandments, so perhaps Orwell's decision to include 'Seven Commandments' is based on his belief they too will be broken by the animals.

As we have seen, Snowball appears to be upholding the tenets of Animalism with his committees, which inevitably fail, like Animalism, because they are too idealistic to be achievable. In the **Motifs** section of the **Language chapter** (above), we explored how Snowball interprets the Seven Commandments for the animals, who struggle to understand them because of their lack of intelligence. By condensing the message to 'Four legs good, two legs bad', Snowball initially appears to be helping the animals to understand the Seven Commandments. Whether intentionally or unintentionally, however, he is making the dull-witted animals more vulnerable: by acting as an intellectual intermediary, Snowball disempowers the animals because he is creating an imbalance of knowledge. When Snowball condenses the Commandments to a single slogan, he focuses their attention on the propaganda message. This diverts their thoughts away from the content of the Seven Commandments, thereby clearing the path for the pigs to implement their own regime.

It is ironic that immediately after the 'Seven Commandments' have been painted on the wall in chapter 2, we see evidence of the corruption of the 'All animals are equal' philosophy. Having already seen Napoleon deliberately stand in front of the buckets before the milk disappears, we have dramatic irony, as the reader deduces what the animals do not know: Napoleon has stolen the milk. This is another hint from Orwell that the totalitarian society is doomed to failure. Napoleon is corrupt. Thus, corruption and the planned exploitation of the animals are seen to exist from the very beginning of the revolution.

The corruption of the pigs is confirmed in chapter 3 when the animals learn that they have taken the 'milk and apples'. In the **THEME: The Power of Language chapter** (above), we examined Squealer's use of pseudo-science to justify this behaviour and to position the pigs as creatures who do not want the 'milk and apples' but who paradoxically take them for the benefit of the other animals. If the animals had at this point challenged the pigs, the situation might never have got out of control—Animal Farm might have evolved into a society adhering to the principles of Animalism. As it is, the pigs get away with stealing resources, and this foreshadows them acquiring later trappings of power such as the farmhouse, whips, clothes and whisky. We therefore have evidence that the pigs are not interested in collectively working for the common good.

In the same chapter, we see the pigs' increasing power as they 'directed and supervised' the harvest, with the other animals doing the hard work. The 'All animals are equal' philosophy becomes steadily less evident as the novella proceeds, and the pigs show themselves to be more interested in taking power than working collectively for the common good.

We see another example of the corruption of communist ideology in chapter 3 when Napoleon exploits the animals' idealism. Mass literacy was an essential part of the post-revolutionary Soviet Union because Lenin wanted an educated populace. The curriculum included atheist instruction, which replaced religious studies. Communist ideology was also integrated into the education system. Napoleon claims that he will be 'responsible' for the 'education' of Jessie and Bluebell's puppies. This initially appears to be a noble act, but we later learn that he has seized the puppies, indoctrinated them and turned them into vicious guard dogs. This is clearly part of Napoleon's plan to seize power. Once more, we see in his devious planning the growing gap between Animalism and the reality of animal/human nature.

At the end of chapter 4, Orwell employs contrast to introduce the worrying idea that one tyrant might replace another. After the Battle of the Cowshed, Boxer is distraught because he thinks he has killed the 'stable-lad'. Orwell employs the word 'lad' to denote that the victim is young and vulnerable; furthermore, Boxer's guilt is deepened because the boy's job is to look after and nurture horses. Boxer's distress foreshadows his inability to survive the harsh regime that will develop at Animal Farm. By way of contrast, the pig Snowball shows no remorse for the stable boy's apparent death, stating 'The only good human being is a dead one'. (To Snowball, if there are deaths in the defence of Animalism, so be it, as he later makes clear at the sheep's funeral.) The contrasting attitudes of Boxer and Snowball to the stable boy show their different levels of empathy. Snowball's belief that all who oppose Animalism should die is another step on the road to the tyranny of the pigs.

At the end of the same chapter, the animals invent military decorations (of different classes, creating yet more distinctions between the animals) and they agree to fire Jones's gun twice a year. Although this appears to be a celebratory ritual, the worrying image of the gun focuses the attention of the reader on the military might of the pigs. Furthermore, because the gun belonged to Mr Jones, its acquisition foreshadows the inevitability of the farm's previous totalitarian regime being replaced by a new one.

Chapter 5 is halfway through the novella and it is here that, should we employ the first model of Freytag's Pyramid, the rising tension finally reaches its climax when Napoleon comes to power. We see this begin to happen at the start of the chapter when the animals agree that the pigs can be responsible for 'all questions of farm policy' although their decisions will still need to be ratified. By the end of the chapter, the falling action has begun. The consequences of Snowball's forced eviction from the farm are that Napoleon now has complete power over the animals; the debates have stopped, so ratification is no longer necessary; and the animals now live under another effectively totalitarian regime.

The dogs play an important role in chapter 5 because they illustrate the rising abuse of power. Jessie and Bluebell's puppies symbolise Stalin's secret service, which eliminated his enemies in his Reign of Terror. They provide evidence that previous claims (usually via Squealer) that Napoleon was working to support the good of the animals and to promote Animalism were a lie. It is also obvious that when Napoleon took Jessie and Bluebell's puppies away in chapter 3, he was planning to train them and seize power all along. This was clearly his long-term plan.

Snowball's abrupt departure when the dogs chase him off the farm symbolises Trotsky's forced exile; it also represents the climax of Napoleon's plans to seize power, making the reader feeling uneasy about the future of the animals. This is the first time in the novella that we see Napoleon use brutality to get his own way, confirming that he is not interested in political debate and that his power is ultimately based on the threat of violence. This mirrors Stalin, who by 1927 had used acts of terror to gain control of the Communist Party. Furthermore, when four pigs attempt to express their disapproval to Napoleon about what has happened, the dogs growl their warnings and the sheep bleat the slogan 'Four legs good, two legs bad!' to drown out objections. By seizing power, threatening violence and not allowing any animals but pigs to vote, Napoleon ensures Animal Farm is no longer based on the ideology of Animalism.

In the **THEME: The Power of Language** chapter, we explored examples of Squealer's propaganda, which he increasingly uses to strengthen Napoleon's power. Squealer's verbal bombardment of the animals accompanies Napoleon's violent behaviour. The former pig's words serve to legitimise the tyrant in the eyes of the animals.

At the beginning of chapter 6, the animals still believe that they are free and working to benefit themselves according to the original principles of Animalism; however, they are deluded. Seeing the world through the rose-tinted spectacles of Animalism, they do not understand the reality of the pigs' power. Orwell opens the chapter with the simple and shocking simile that the animals are working 'like slaves'. They have no freedom, as their lives are completely controlled by the pigs. It is ironic that whilst they are relieved they are not working for 'a pack of idle, thieving human beings', they do not see that they are working just as hard—if not harder—for the cruel and exploitative pigs. The farm's reality is not what it appears to be.

Napoleon manipulates the principles of Animalism when he says that the animals must work on Sundays, but that this is 'strictly voluntary': the reader sees the irony in this statement because Napoleon threatens to reduce rations for those who do not volunteer. This coercion reflects the apparently voluntary work programmes in the Stalinist Soviet Union, which in reality were forced labour. It is in the interests of Napoleon to keep the animals hard at work and co-operative, as they are less likely to challenge his rule.

Orwell explores the idea of self-sacrifice as a tool of power when Napoleon aligns himself with Boxer. Earlier in the novella, Squealer announced that the pigs did not like 'milk and apples', but were consuming them because they contained the essential goodness needed to run the farm and therefore help the animals; similarly, in chapter 6, Napoleon announces that he will shoulder the 'burden' of forming trade alliances with the humans, even though the creation of these alliances is contrary to the self-sufficiency principles of Animalism. Napoleon suggests that dealing with humans is as hard and unpleasant for him as hauling stones is for Boxer (whose philosophy is to 'work harder'). Napoleon does this to communicate to the animals that he is also sacrificing himself for the greater good. The reader can see, however, the difference between the falseness of Napoleon and the genuine selflessness of Boxer.

Orwell develops the concept of 'sacrifice' to draw the attention of the reader to the appearance of Animalism versus and the reality of living under a totalitarian regime. In chapter 6, Napoleon states that the hens 'should welcome this sacrifice' of their eggs, which he wants to use in trade. The astute reader will at this point remember that old Major used the example of Mr Jones selling the hens' eggs as one of his many reasons to encourage the rebellion. By promoting the idea of 'sacrifice' for the benefit of Animalism, we therefore see the hypocrisy of Napoleon's words and, by default, Orwell's view that totalitarian regimes are hypocritical.

As with chapter 6, much of the focus of chapter 7 is on the totalitarian regime and its violence towards the animals. This is the falling action that follows the climax of Snowball's exile; the fact that such violence is part of the falling action rather than the rising action or the climax underscores the horror of the totalitarian regime's abuse of power. To maintain his power, Napoleon eliminates any serious opposition because the failure so far of the windmill means that the pigs are vulnerable to another revolution. The alleged confessions, followed swiftly by executions, therefore instil a terrified subservience to Napoleon/Stalin. During the 1930s, Stalin arrested and tortured his enemies on the flimsiest of evidence, denouncing them as 'enemies of the people'. This was a convenient way to eliminate high-ranking political and military threats and to make everyone fear for their safety; therefore, they were more likely to obey him and follow orders.

Orwell also illustrates how totalitarian regimes manipulate their population by creating a convenient common enemy: Napoleon uses Snowball as a scapegoat so that when things go wrong at the farm, attention is deflected from the leader. We have seen how Snowball was blamed for the failure of the windmill—then in chapter 7, the animals' thoughts are manipulated further by the 'documents' that allegedly prove that Snowball is in league with Jones. The noun 'documents' is an official sounding word that suggests the idea of formal correspondence. The choice of word is likely to intimidate the animals with their limited reading skills, and they are less likely to challenge the pigs by asking to read them. The pigs therefore exploit the animals' lack of education to justify their rule.

The idea of conditioning people's thoughts by depriving them of the means to read and access other views or even to express their own views can be seen at the end of chapter 7. Clover reflects on old Major's dream for the farm, but she is unable to articulate 'the words to express' her thoughts: now that the animals are no longer being educated, they are deprived of the means to articulate their ideas. This is like the 'thought control' in Orwell's next novel, *Nineteen Eighty-Four*, in which the state by various means—including education, propaganda and torture—breaks down people's capacity for independent thought, thereby removing any threat to the regime.

We learn that a capacity for independent thought can make an animal a target of Napoleon's tyranny. Boxer, as we have seen, is blindly loyal. Although he does not initially believe Squealer's story about Snowball, he is prepared to believe Napoleon's version of history more than his own memories ('Napoleon is always right'). Nevertheless, despite Boxer believing the new 'truth' about Snowball, the fact that he voices memories that contradict the official party line turns him into a threat.

We see in chapter 8 that the pigs are literally rewriting the Commandments when 'No animal shall kill any other animal' becomes 'No animal shall kill any other animal WITHOUT CAUSE'. The amendment 'WITHOUT CAUSE' justifies the killings in the minds of the animals—after all, Napoleon decides whether he has cause to kill other animals and, as mentioned above, 'Napoleon is always right.' The additional detail 'with sheets' is added to the Commandment 'No animal shall sleep in a bed' while 'to excess' is added to 'No animal shall drink alcohol'. In all cases, the later amendments aim to excuse Napoleon's tyrannical behaviour and to legitimise his actions. We also see that power corrupts its possessors because the changes to the commandments are for the sole benefit of the pigs.

It has already been mentioned that at the end of chapter 8 the animals find the unconscious Squealer next to a ladder and pot of paint: now, the reader sees the full impact that the totalitarian regime has had on the animals. Despite the evidence in front of their eyes, the animals still cannot see that the pigs have been abusing their power by changing the commandments. In any case, apart from Benjamin, the animals lack the intelligence to challenge the changes.

Also in chapter 8, we see more corruption of the socialist idea of equality, as the gulf between the classes grows even wider. Even between the pigs, there is now a hierarchy: Napoleon is rarely seen in public; a black cockerel announces his occasional appearances; he lives apart from the other pigs; he eats from Mr Jones's expensive crockery; he orders that the gun is to be fired to celebrate his birthday; he is given more titles; he tells Minimus to write the poem about him on the barn wall; a pig test-tastes his food for poison; he names the windmill after himself; and the animals have to walk in front of him to admire the money from the sale of the wood while he reclines next to it. By describing in such detail these developments in Napoleon's behaviour, Orwell draws the reader's attention to the importance of image and how it can be a tool to manipulate the animals. Orwell is also providing the reader with evidence that Animalism or communism do not work.

Orwell uses the symbolism of the 'whisky' to illustrate that the pigs are —in terms of their behaviour and attitudes to the animals—resembling more and more the masters they replaced. The reader compares the drunken Napoleon to the drunken Mr Jones and concludes that Napoleon is just as self-serving and irresponsible. Unlike Jones and the humans, however, the pigs are inexperienced with the effects of excessive alcohol intake. When the animals mistakenly believe that Napoleon's overindulgence has resulted in death, the 'whisky' becomes a symbol of the pigs' real feelings towards the animals. Unlike the animals who fought and died for the cause of Animalism, Napoleon's seeming death is self-inflicted because of self-indulgence and gluttony, appropriate for a pig. The apparent death of Napoleon dishonours the 'real' dead who have sacrificed their lives for the farm; moreover, they are drunk at Boxer's memorial, which shows their lack of respect for the horse. It is also implied that Napoleon's decision to have the retirement paddock ploughed up to grow barley is because the fermented mash of barley is used to make whisky: Napoleon prioritises alcohol and profits over the animals. His relationship with the whisky therefore reveals the leader's lack of interest in the animals and his indifference to their welfare.

In chapter 9, Napoleon once again widens the class divisions between the pigs and the other animals with his treatment of the piglets. Not only are they to be educated separately and discouraged from playing with the other animals, but also new rules are introduced about stepping away from an approaching pig. Orwell employs the ribbon motif to emphasise these differences: pigs can wear 'green ribbons' on Sundays. The astute reader will recall the symbolism of Molly's ribbons, previously dismissed as vain and self-indulgent. The pigs are therefore becoming more and more like the elitist regime they have replaced.

In the same chapter, the reader sees with the fate of Boxer the widescale corruption of the totalitarian regime. We read about Boxer's slow decline in health and then, towards the end of the chapter, Orwell describes in detail the manner of his departure in the knacker's van. Sandwiched in between, Orwell focuses the attention of the reader on the reduced rations for the animals and the increasing power of the pigs. This emphasises the class divisions and makes the description of Boxer's final journey more harrowing and believable.

Orwell uses Boxer's death to suggest how little Stalin valued his people and that ultimately, he betrayed them. Boxer is loyal but dim-witted, symbolising the Soviet workers who unquestioningly and blindly followed Stalin. In chapter 9, we see that Boxer has fallen victim to his 'I will work harder' ethic by working himself nearly to death. His relentless work habit illustrates how, despite all the evidence that Animalism does not work, he is unable to understand; he does not grasp that he is living once more in a totalitarian society, a society that he himself has helped to create by unquestioningly following the pigs' orders. There is a painful irony in the way that the brainwashed horse has worked for the principles of Animalism and the good of all, only to have the corrupt few at the top benefit from his labour and finally betray him by selling his body for glue and monetary gain. Boxer's death reminds us of the plight of the Soviet workers, many of whom had made sacrifices during the Russian Revolution and on the Eastern Front fighting against Germany. As the quality of life for many loyal Soviet workers became worse, the quality of life for those at the top improved. Orwell is therefore using Boxer's last day to highlight the widening divisions between the classes and to suggest that those at the top have betrayed the workers and the principles of communism.

Boxer's final actions and fate are deeply ironic. When at last he realises what is happening, he tries to kick open the doors and sides of the van to escape, but his giant frame lacks the strength. The regime has taken the best of him, and he has allowed them to take power. This, says Orwell, is the consequence of blind loyalty and of not holding those in power accountable for their actions. The irony is that Boxer has sacrificed his strength for the pigs, and they now sacrifice him for their benefit.

PIGS AS MEN

The falling action leads to the dénouement in chapter 10; here the new habits of the pigs (such as wearing clothes, buying a radio, having a telephone installed, and reading newspapers and magazines) confirm their rapidly increasing similarity to their human predecessors, the Jones family. When they begin to wear the clothes of Mr and Mrs Jones, the pigs are symbolically replacing one totalitarian regime with another. This idea is developed when the neighbouring farmers tour the farm and the animals do not know whether they should be more frightened by the humans or the pigs, foreshadowing the very end of the chapter when we learn that the communist pigs are indistinguishable from the capitalist humans. In the Soviet Union, Stalin and those in his inner circle likewise resembled the overthrown tsar and aristocrats.

We have seen in the **Language** chapter (above) that Orwell's simple journalistic writing style focuses the attention of the reader on the message of his allegory. In chapter 10, he draws attention to how the pigs have betrayed Animalism ideology and violated the commandments through his use of paragraphs of simple sentences. Having been indoctrinated with the slogan 'Four legs good, two legs bad!', Orwell's use of the single paragraph 'It was a pig walking on his hind legs' heightens the impact of the animals' shock. This is an unfortunate image for the reader because it is so unexpected and bizarre, hence comical. For the gullible animals, however, their shock is heightened with the parallel simple-sentence paragraph: 'He carried a whip in his trotter.' The 'whip' of course symbolises the oppression and tyranny of the old regime at the hands of humans who enslaved and maltreated the animals. These visual images combine with the aural bombardment of the sheep's incessant bleating the 'Four legs good, two legs BETTER!' slogan to drown out all possibility of thought and animal reaction. The reader, however, appreciates the hypocrisy of a regime in which the pigs can do exactly what they want; unlike the animals, the reader can judge the developments on the farm in a detached, reflective and intelligent manner.

In the final chapter of the novella, we see that the pigs have abused their power through logic and language to reduce the Commandments of Animalism to a declarative sentence:

ALL ANIMALS ARE EQUAL

BUT SOME ANIMALS ARE MORE EQUAL THAN OTHERS

We see how language aims to manipulate thought when the pigs rewrite the Commandments. The capitalisation of the letters creates an assertive, aggressive tone: disbelieve at your peril. The first independent clause of the compound sentence appears to uphold the tenets of Animalism; however, the co-ordinating conjunction 'BUT' introduces a contradictory point in the second independent clause which implies that there are different levels of equality. This is logically impossible: equality means being the same or equal. The determiner 'some' implies that an elite group exists—those who rule above the others. We therefore see the extent to which the Animalism ideology of old Major has been corrupted, just as Marx's communist ideology was corrupted by Stalin. The original ideology of the farm is no longer recognisable, confirming that the pigs have replaced Mr Jones with another tyrant.

Orwell brings the novella round in full circle to encourage the reader to reflect upon the nature of totalitarian rule. In Napoleon's speech to the farmers in chapter 10, we learn about his decision to ban the noun 'comrade', which was initially introduced by old Major in chapter 1 to create feelings of unity. The reader sees that the animals are truly living under a dictatorship that does not follow the ideology of Animalism because it no longer wishes to create feelings of unity.

This is further emphasised when the pigs decide to change the name 'Animal Farm' back to its original form, 'Manor Farm'. This symbolises the cyclical nature of tyranny, as the farm has now become the totalitarian regime against which the animals rebelled in the first place. It no longer represents a haven for the animals such as Clover who should have retired and yet, like other older animals, still works and falsely believes that she is free. The animals will continue to be exploited, and they will work until they can work no more.

THEME: CLASS STRUCTURES

We discussed earlier how different characters in *Animal Farm* represent different elements of the Soviet population; in particular, how Mr Jones and then the pigs stand for the ruling classes. Class structure is an important theme: it is perfectly obvious by now that Animalism does not work. This poses the question: why? The simple answer is that it has not worked because the animals allowed the pigs to take control. For example, the regular Sunday Meeting for planning and debating described in chapter 3 reflects the socialist principles of equality, yet it is significant that the pigs dominate the meetings. The other animals do not exercise their equal rights: because of their passivity, they allow the pigs to rise to power.

Furthermore, we learn in the same chapter that the pigs are the only animals to show a voracious enthusiasm for education. Many of the other animals are apathetic: the dogs are only interested in reading the Seven Commandments; Benjamin can read but will not; Boxer and Clover try but struggle; Mollie refuses to learn any letters but those of her name; and the rest of the animals get no further than the letter A. We should not criticise any of the animals who lack intelligence. The point is that the pigs exploit the animals' apathy, and this is another reason for their rise to power.

Let's explore the animals (the Russian population) who allowed Napoleon/Stalin's to rise to power:

BENJAMIN

Donkeys are known for their stubbornness and Benjamin is very stubborn. His name is prefixed with the adjective 'old' five times in the novella (compared to seven with old Major). Orwell emphasises the donkey's age to draw an interesting comparison with old Major. The wise and elderly pig formulated and shared the philosophy of Animalism, a philosophy derived partly from his own experience. Benjamin, whilst clever and capable, is not like old Major—he is too detached. He remembers the past, can speculate accurately about the future and has, in his own opinion, seen everything. This has resulted in a cynicism that renders all action ultimately pointless. For example, he 'could read as well as any pig, but never exercised his faculty' because there is 'nothing worth reading'. This cynicism also applies to the windmill, to Animalism, and even to his best friend Boxer. Benjamin probably understands that the van is not there to take Boxer to the hospital, but he does nothing to save his friend until it is too late.

When the animals ask him about the rebellion, he states mysteriously 'Donkeys live a long time'. In other words, he has seen it all before and is aware that the pigs will probably abuse their power. With his lack of enthusiasm for Animalism, Benjamin represents the passive bystander who does nothing to stop the pigs' rise to power.

Unlike Major the idealist, Benjamin is both a pessimist and a realist. In chapter 5, he refuses to vote for Napoleon or Snowball, stating 'Life would go on as it had always gone on—that is, badly'. At the end of the day, he is right, as the animals end as they began, living in a totalitarian society. Nevertheless, Orwell stresses that intellectually he is the pigs' equal with his reading skills. Morally, Benjamin is responsible for the pigs' rise to power because he could have challenged the totalitarian regime, roused the animals to action and stopped the pigs from rising to power.

BOXER

Boxer symbolises the loyal, hard-working proletariat who supported the Russian Revolution. Carthorses are known for their strength, a quality that we see reflected in Boxer's name: a boxer is a strong fighter, who faces adversity. His ideas are also boxed in because he has simple-minded, unquestioning loyalty to communist ideas. His lack of intelligence makes it easy for the pigs to manipulate him—his work ethic of 'I will work harder' marks him as the perfect loyal, exploitable worker. He is easy to lead and to control. His historical counterpart is a miner called Alexei Stakhanov, who in one shift is said to have mined fourteen times the amount of coal expected from one person. Unlike Boxer, who is admired by the animals, Stakhanov was unpopular with his fellow miners because they were expected to work as hard as him.

By chapter 5, the propaganda is clearly working on all the animals except Benjamin; it works most effectively on Boxer, who represents the unflagging devotion of the workers in the cause of communism. He appears to be incapable of independent thought, mindlessly thinking in slogans such as 'I will work harder' and 'Napoleon is always right'. Orwell's use of slogans emphasises the horse's lack of independent thought and therefore his inability to challenge Napoleon's rule. We see once more the power of language, as slogans serve to control the thoughts and actions of the populace.

Boxer's death and its significance are discussed in detail in the previous chapter under **The Pigs** subheading.

CAT

Rarely mentioned, the cat is lazy and indifferent to politics on the farm, voting on both sides of the question about whether the rats are 'comrades'. We see a comic moment when the cat joins the re-education committee and tries to persuade the sparrows that she will not harm them (the reader suspects that the sparrows are right to mistrust her). This failure in her role might represent the laziness and apathy of some members of the Russian population.

CLOVER

Clover represents the loyal, hard-working female proletariat of the Soviet Union. She is 'a stout motherly mare approaching middle life, who had never quite got her figure back after her fourth foal'. Being a 'motherly' figure suggests that Clover is stereotyped as a worrier and nurturer. She looks after the ducklings at Major's meeting; she is suspicious of Mollie in chapter 5 but chooses not to report her; and she worries about Boxer. Because she places others first, she can be vulnerable and is therefore the opposite of Benjamin. As well as focusing on her maternal attributes, Orwell's description centres on her appearance, which renders her problematic and unsympathetic in the eyes of contemporary female readers. Orwell is, however, echoing a point made by Lenin about women in society. At the First All-Russia Congress of Working Women in 1918, Lenin stated: 'The status of women up to now has been compared to that of a slave; women have been tied to the home, and only socialism can save them from this. They will only be completely emancipated when we change from small-scale individual farming to collective farming and collective working of the land'. In other words, women should free themselves from the home and get a job working on the land. To facilitate this (and thereby increase the labour force), laws were passed after the Russian Revolution to grant women equal status to men. The reality was, however, that freedom from home and hearth did not entirely arrive, despite Lenin and Stalin's actions.

Interestingly, we learn that Clover is slightly cleverer than her companion Boxer because she learnt the whole alphabet (but she could not make words with the letters). Perhaps Orwell is making the point that with access to education some women have the potential to exceed the attainment of men. Nevertheless, like Boxer, she initially believes everything that the pigs say, and she is gullible. In this respect, she represents the millions of Russian women who believed the socialist message.

Clover also represents the population that remembers life before the Revolution. Consequently, they know or suspect that the government is lying to them, but they are helpless to change anything. For example, Clover suspects that something is wrong when the pigs begin to change the Seven Commandments, but she cannot be sure as she cannot read. When Muriel reads to Clover, she begins to believe that the changes have always been there. Once the executions begin, Clover becomes tearful because she knows that the principles of Animalism are being violated. Yet she accepts Napoleon's leadership and is not clever enough or sufficiently rebellious enough to challenge him.

DOGS

There are three sheepdogs on the farm: Jessie, Bluebell and Pincher. Jessie, intelligent and enquiring, is the first to notice that something is not right with the pigs. After she and Bluebell have litters, Napoleon steals all nine puppies. We later see them as his secret police or, to place them in the historical context, Stalin's secret police who killed anyone who opposed him. Their role is discussed in more detail in the previous chapter.

OLD MAJOR

As we have seen, old Major represents the founding fathers of communism, Marx and Engels. The significance of his character and speech has been analysed in the **THEME: The Power of Language** chapter.

Some animals, blinded by Major's impassioned rhetoric, do not understand his socialist ideas; others naively buy into his vision of a utopian society. Intellectually, the pigs are superior: they are quickly able to subvert Animalism while other animals (with the possible exception of Benjamin) do not. The growing differences between the pigs and the other animals are described in the previous chapter.

MOLLIE

Orwell depicts Mollie as a materialist who loves sugar and ribbons; she prefers a more pampered lifestyle and who puts her own needs first. Mollie represents White Russians (dispossessed landowners, factory owners, members of the church and royalists) who supported the tsar and emigrated from the Soviet Union around the time of the Russian Civil War. Her love of ribbons is discussed in the *Motifs* section of the **Language** chapter, above.

Orwell parodies Mollie's vanity in chapter 3 when she is reluctant to work and refuses to learn any other letters but the ones that spell her name. She is not interested in politics and comes across as childish and vain, acting only in her own self-interest. She puts her needs before those of anyone else, frequently being late for work. Likewise, the White Russians were perceived by the Bolsheviks to be putting their needs above those of the nation; for example, after the revolution, landowners wanted their land to be returned to them. Unlike many White Russians who were prepared to fight for their cause, Mollie hides behind the cowshed in The Battle of the Cowshed. Not only does this illustrate her lack of support for the Animalist cause, but it also stresses her superficiality: she desires an easy life but is not prepared to fight for it.

Orwell suggests that Mollie is better off after her defection. The pigeons report: 'She appeared to be enjoying herself'. She is not interested in politics and was not motivated by politics to defect—simply her own material well-being. Orwell poses the interesting question of whether it is better to emigrate and make a new life or to stay and suffer with your friends.

MURIEL

Muriel the goat is intelligent and learns to read. We see that she has the brains to challenge Napoleon's rise to power but, like Benjamin, she does nothing. She therefore represents those who support the rebellion and do nothing to stop the increasing exploitation of the population, choosing to take a minor role.

PIGEONS

The pigeons serve as spies. They are ordered to fly to neighbouring farms to teach the animals about the revolution on Animal Farm and the 'Beasts of England' anthem in the hope that knowledge of both will incite further rebellions. They represent the *Comintern* (the *Communist Internationale*), which was created by Lenin in 1919 to encourage world revolution. Like the pigeons, members of *Comintern*, spread Soviet propaganda to other countries.

In chapter 8, Napoleon uses the pigeons to spread conflicting propaganda; for example, he orders them to say, 'Death to Frederick' and then to change this to 'Death to Pilkington'. These carefully controlled slogans are dutifully spread by the pigeons. Orwell illustrates here how the Soviet regime was prepared to reverse statements, so its propaganda was not to be trusted.

SHEEP

The simple-minded sheep lack individual names: they represent the unthinking masses who follow strong leaders, unquestioningly doing as they are told, blindly repeating 'Four legs good, two legs bad' throughout the novella. They are a useful tool for Napoleon, particularly when there are disagreements and the sheep shout down the dissenters. They are so simple-minded that they have no rational arguments to contribute, simply repeating 'Four legs good, two legs bad' or, by the end of the novella, 'Four legs good, two legs better'.

THEME: International Alliances

We have already explored the character of Mr Jones, who represents Tsar Nicholas II while Mrs Jones represents Empress Alexandra. The other humans also have a symbolic purpose, and the pigs' interactions with them represent international alliances or conflict.

Chapter 4 sees Mr Jones in the pub, complaining about his plight; primarily, his character represents Tsar Nicholas II, but at this moment in the novella he symbolises anti-communist forces talking to the Allied Interventionist Nations. The Allies were suspicious of communism because it posed a threat to their own regimes—they were keenly aware that one communist uprising might trigger others. Communism was therefore regarded as a serious threat. Pilkington (from Foxwood) and Frederick (from Pinchfield) deliberately invent lies about torture and other horrors at Animal Farm, and these lies represent the West's anti-communist propaganda.

Neither Pilkington nor Frederick is depicted by Orwell to be worthy of farm ownership, and we must consider the reasons why. Pilkington's farm is in a 'disgraceful condition' and Frederick is 'perpetually involved in lawsuits'. These neglectful and quarrelsome attitudes contrast with the mutually supportive ideology of Animalism. We know that Orwell was sceptical about the reality of socialist regimes; perhaps he positions the selfishness of capitalism against communism to imply that neither has much to recommend it, evidenced at the end of the novella when we see the pigs replace their capitalist master.

When Jones (along with men from Foxwood and Pinchfield farms) attempts to regain control of Animal Farm in chapter 4, this action mirrors the multinational North Russian Intervention Allies invading the Soviet Union in October 1918. The purpose of the unsuccessful invasion was to remove Lenin and the communist government from power. Trotsky, the leader of Lenin's Red Army, proved to be a great strategist; in Orwell's version, Snowball directs the animals in 'The Battle of the Cowshed' with similar success.

The war between the Red Army (communists) and the White Army (anti-communist Allies) lasted for two years. When the Red Army under the leadership of Trotsky won, the communists' hold on the Soviet Union was consolidated, just as the animals' hold on Animal Farm is strengthened. The profound irony of 'The Battle of the Cowshed' is the way that it illustrates the gap between what the animals believe they are fighting for and the reality of their situation. The animals believe that they are defending Animalism and protecting themselves from the return of Mr Jones's totalitarian regime; however, by eliminating an external threat to the pigs' new regime, the animals are really consolidating the pigs' power.

In chapter 6, the pigs employ Mr Whymper, who represents outsiders who support the Russian Revolution. His historical parallel is a *Comintern* foreign agent (as opposed to Soviet agents like the pigeons). The pigs tell Mr Whymper a series of lies and deceptions about Animal Farm's progress so that he will unwittingly spread these falsehoods to the outside world. In chapter 7, the pigs want to convince Mr. Whymper that they have enough food and are thriving. Napoleon is the director of the show; the sheep are given lines to recite about the increasing rations; and the sand and grain bins are props. This staging symbolises the corruption within the Soviet regime, and once again Orwell shows that propaganda cannot be trusted.

Mr Pilkington comes to represents the Allies while Mr Frederick represents Hitler or Nazi Germany. This explains why they 'disliked each other' and 'it was difficult for them to come to any agreement, even in defence of their own interests' (chapter 4). The episode in chapter 8 with Napoleon wavering between selling the pile of wood to Pilkington or to Frederick symbolises Stalin's negotiations with the capitalist Allies and the fascist Hitler before World War II. Reluctant to enter a war, Stalin stalled them by favouring one side and then another. Each time, he would use propaganda to criticise the opposing side and to influence his people. When Napoleon eventually decides to sell the wood to Frederick, this parallels the Non-Aggression Pact between Stalin and Hitler in 1939 in which Germany promised not to invade the Soviet Union. In 1941, Germany broke the pact and invaded Russia; this is paralleled within the text when Frederick (Hitler) pays Napoleon in counterfeit money, symbolising Hitler's lies.

In the final chapter of the novella, Pilkington's comment to Napoleon that 'you have your lower animals to contend with' and 'we have our lower classes!' makes it very clear that all totalitarian governments are the same. Both leaders oppress and exploit their workers to maintain their own power. Pilkington's remark reduces human workers to the level of animal workers, revealing the attitude that they are there to be exploited. This makes the reader appreciate that the consequences of communism are terrifying: this might not be a fairy story. This could be real life. This could be a story about humans, not animals.

The meeting between Pilkington and Napoleon mirrors the Tehran Conference in 1943 at which Stalin, Winston Churchill and Franklin D. Roosevelt met to discuss how they could ensure peace after the war. Napoleon and Pilkington's argument in the card game symbolises that peace would not possible, hence the future Cold War. The argument also symbolises the similar self-interests of the pigs and humans. Like Mr Jones, the pigs now carry whips, drink, smoke, kill, lie and cheat to further their aims. The worst of human nature dominates their thoughts and actions, emphasising that, if left alone with this central weakness, the dream represented by Animalism is bound to fail.

Useful Quotations

The quotations that follow are useful because they link to a variety of characters, themes, contextual elements, language and structural features. You are not expected to remember all of them, so highlight half a dozen or so that you feel you can memorise easily and just read the others.

The examiner is looking for:

1. Short quotations worked into your own sentences
2. Relevant textual references. A relevant textual reference means to paraphrase a quotation if you cannot remember the exact words.

Both sorts of comment should be worked into the flow of your own sentences for maximum impact.

Quotation	Character	Theme/Comment
'too drunk to remember to shut the pop-holes'	Mr Jones	Tyranny & historical counterpart (the tsar) Language analysis Abuse of power
'lurched'	Mr Jones	Language analysis Abuse of power
'fox in the yard'	Mr Jones	Language analysis Tyranny Context
'old'	1. Old Major 2. Benjamin	1. Suggests wisdom and life experience to formulate Animalism ideology 2. Also suggests life experience Contrast with Major: cynical and detached
'Animalism'	Old Major	Communism ideology, based on *Communist Manifesto* written by Marx and Engels
'raised platform' 'front'	Major sits on this Pigs and dogs at front	Visual symbolism of status Animalism will fail
'Comrades' 'friends' 'you and I'	Old Major	Language analysis: inclusive terms of address Propaganda
'what is the nature of this life of ours?'	Old Major	Language analysis Structure: rhetoric Animalism
'the life of an animal is misery and slavery' 'like slaves'	Old Major's speech Chapter 6	Emotive language Echoes *Communist Manifesto* (see ***Animal Farm* and Historical Parallels**, chapter 2) Analyse the simile: life under new regime has not changed. Irony: animals think it has
'Man is the only creature that consumes without producing.'	Old Major's speech	Echoes *Communist Manifesto* (see ***Animal Farm* and Historical Parallels**, chapter 2)

Quotation	Character	Theme/Comment
'He does not give milk, he does not lay eggs' 'Yet he is lord of all the animals.'	Old Major's speech	Language analysis: parallelism Simple sentence for emphasis. Class Abuse of power Exploitation Foreshadowing
'All animals are equal.' 'ALL ANIMALS ARE EQUAL / BUT SOME ANIMALS ARE MORE EQUAL THAN OTHERS'.	Old Major's speech Final chapter	Seven Commandments have been reduced Echoes *Communist Manifesto* (see *Animal Farm* and Historical Parallels, chapter 2) Breakdown of Animalism Hypocrisy Language analysis
'-Man. Man is the only real enemy we have. Remove man from the scene, and the root cause of hunger and overwork is abolished for ever'.	Old Major's speech	Echoes *Communist Manifesto* (see *Animal Farm* and Historical Parallels, chapter 2) Language analysis of metaphor
'cruel knife' 'horror' 'scream'	Old Major's speech	Language analysis: personification and emotive language Rhetoric Class Tyranny and abuse of power Foreshadowing
'All men are enemies. All animals are comrades' 'rats'	Old Major's speech	Animalism Context Juxtaposition & situational irony
'Rebellion!'	Old Major's speech	Echoes *Communist Manifesto* (see *Animal Farm* and Historical Parallels, chapter 2)
'Beasts of England'	Old Major teaches this to the animals.	Anthem becomes a communist propaganda tool Napoleon forbids it
'fruitful fields' 'golden future time'	Words in 'Beasts of England'	Language analysis Unachievable dream like Animalism
'Manor Farm' 'Animal Farm'	Snowball repaints the name. Napoleon changes it back to original.	Symbolism of setting Cyclical structure of novella & the cyclical nature of tyranny

Quotation	Character	Theme/Comment
'Seven Commandments'	Created by pigs	No consultation with animals about the Commandments violates Animalism ideology
		Each Commandment is broken, reflecting breakdown of Animalism. Context: Ten Commandments
'it was noticed that the milk had disappeared'	Animals notice this	Use of passive voice
		Animals could have challenged this but did not
		First sign of pigs' abuse of power
'Four legs good, two legs bad.'	Snowball interprets Seven Commandments for the animals.	Sheep bleat this to interrupt Snowball's speeches
		Role of slogans in propaganda
		Animals focus on this, rather than the Seven Commandments, making them vulnerable
		Pigs' rise to power
		Corruption of Animalism
		Bombarding animals with words to stop free thinking and debates.
'Four legs good, two legs better.'	Sheep	Symbolises breakdown of Animalism and hypocrisy of pigs.
		Sheep do not question the change.
'Sugarcandy Mountain'	Moses the raven	Religion and relationship with state
		Propaganda
'The Battle of the Cowshed'		Communist victory against the anti-communist Allies
		Napoleon/Trotsky as a tactician
'Windmill'		Symbolism of setting
'The Battle of the Windmill'		German invasion of Russia in 1941.
'Napoleon Mill'		Propaganda.
		Stalin's cult of personality.
'Barn'		Symbolism of setting
'No animal shall drink alcohol.' 'No animal shall drink alcohol to excess.'	One of the Seven Commandments Rewritten Commandment	Animalism
		Totalitarian rule
		Napoleon
		Hypocrisy
		Abuse of power
'Hams' 'chasing him round and round a bonfire when he was suffering from a cough'	Confessions and executions	Language analysis of humour
		Power and abuse of power
		Tyranny/Terror
		Failure of Animalism
'Animal Farm, Animal Farm, Never through me shalt thou come to harm!'	Song composed by Minimus to replace 'Beasts of England'	Language analysis
		Situational irony
		Propaganda
		Context: propaganda controls art

Quotation	Character	Theme/Comment
'Thou watchest over all' 'Lord of the swill-bucket!'	Minimus's poem entitled 'Comrade Napoleon'	Language analysis Napoleon & cult of personality Humour Propaganda
'hoof and horn' 'Order of the Green Banner' 'more songs, more speeches, more processions' 'spontaneous demonstration'		Rituals and ceremonies Propaganda Soviet context Power and control Language analysis Irony
'I will work harder' 'Napoleon is always right.'	Boxer	His character (context & class) His exploitation by Soviet regime.
'Ribbons' 'Sugar'	Mollie	Symbolism of her character (context & class) Symbolism of objects
'green ribbons'	Pigs	Hypocrisy Corruption of Animalism Class
'She appeared to be enjoying herself'	Pigeons report this about Mollie after she defects	Mollie and her function Context: White Russians Rejection of Animalism Class
'bowler hat'	Mr Jones Napoleon knacker	Motif & symbolism Tyranny and abuse of power Class
'whip' 'He carried a whip in his trotter.'	Mr Jones knacker Napoleon	Motif Language analysis and symbolism Tyranny and abuse of power Class
'milk and apples'	Napoleon	Animalism Abuse of power
'directed and supervised'	Pigs did this to animals when they were bringing in the harvest	Animalism Class
'all questions of farm policy'	Pigs decide this	Breakdown of Animalism Class Power
'turn black into white'	Squealer	Language analysis Propaganda Soviet context
'skipping from side to side'	Squealer	Language analysis Propaganda
'science' 'Jones would come back!' 'tactics'	Squealer	Language analysis of persuasive techniques Propaganda
'Then we have won back what we had before.'	Boxer after The Battle of the Windmill	Unusually perceptive comment about meaningless propaganda by the normally slow-witted carthorse

Quotation	Character	Theme/Comment
'readjustment'	Squealer about cuts to rations	Propaganda Language analysis of euphemism
'Republic' 'President' 'elected'	Napoleon	Corruption of power Tyranny Class Irony
'No animal shall sleep in a bed' 'No animal shall sleep in a bed with sheets'	Seven Commandments Pigs	Corruption of Animalism Pigs Class Abuse of power
'bread soaked in beer' 'beer'	Mr Jones fed this to Moses Pigs give this to Moses	Corruption Religion and propaganda Power Context & Russian Orthodox Church
'argue very hard'	Pigs against Moses	Context & Russian Orthodox Church
'lies' (noun)	Pigs do not believe Moses but allow him to talk to animals	Corruption Religion and propaganda Power Context & Russian Orthodox Church
'fierce'	Napoleon	Language analysis
'disliked each other' 'it was difficult for them to come to any agreement, even in defence of their own interests'	Pilkington & Frederick	Symbolism of names (see **International Alliances** chapter) Context Power
'disgraceful condition' 'perpetually involved in lawsuits'	Foxwood Farm Frederick	Owned by Pilkington Symbolism of name Owns Pinchfield Farm Symbolism of name Orwell's view of capitalists Symbolism of the characters
'Wild Comrade's Re-education Committee'	Cat to sparrows	Humour and irony Animalism does not work
'stable-lad' 'The only good human being is a dead one'	Boxer Snowball	Battle of the Cowshed Language analysis of contrast Sacrifices for power Animalism
'bitterly hard'	The weather in chapter 5	Pathetic fallacy: Snowball and Napoleon's relationship
'brilliant speeches'	Snowball	Trotsky Rhetoric Power of language Animalism

Quotation	Character	Theme/Comment
'more vivacious' 'quicker in speech and more inventive'	Snowball	Trotsky Comparison with Napoleon/Stalin Link to Animalism ideology: windmill, debates, etc.
'documents'	Squealer	Rhetoric Abuse of power Language analysis
'the words to express'	Clover	Power of language Education Control
'No animal shall kill any other animal.' 'No animal shall kill any other animal WITHOUT CAUSE.'	Seven Commandments	Animalism Communism Tyranny Abuse of power Context: Great Purges/Terror
'Whisky'	Mr Jones Pigs	Symbolism Tyranny Abuse of power Class
'responsible' 'education'	Napoleon will be 'responsible' for the 'education' of Jessie and Bluebell's puppies.	Class Tyranny and abuse of power Context: Stalin & secret police
'burden'	Napoleon will shoulder the 'burden' of forming trade alliances with the humans.	Napoleon Decline of Animalism. Language analysis
'strictly voluntary'	Napoleon tells animals they must work on Sundays or their rations will be cut.	Language analysis Propaganda and irony Napoleon Tyranny and abuse of power Context: forced labour was claimed to be voluntary. Five-Year plans.
'should welcome this sacrifice'	Napoleon to hens about their eggs	Decline of Animalism Tyranny and abuse of power
'It was a pig walking on his hind legs.' 'He carried a whip in his trotter'	Napoleon	Tyranny Class End of Animalism Symbolism & sentence type (simple) in own paragraph.
'nothing worth reading' 'Donkeys live a long time' 'Life would go on as it had always gone on—that is, badly' 'could read as well as any pig, but never exercised his faculty'	Benjamin	Comparison with old Major Function of his character Class View of tyranny & Animalism Irony: he could have agitated against the rise of the pigs to power

Quotation	Character	Theme/Comment
'a stout motherly mare approaching middle life, who had never quite got her figure back after her fourth foal'	Clover	Symbolism of her character and function Class and gender roles Lenin's speech at First All-Russia Congress of Working Women in 1918.
'Death to Frederick' 'Death to Pilkington'	Pigeons under orders from pigs	Propaganda Animalism International context
'you have your lower animals to contend with' 'we have our lower classes!'	Pilkington to pigs	Tyranny and abuse of power Class End of Animalism Context: Tehran Conference, 1943

Example Essay

You might feel that the essay below is rather long for the time provided in the exam. This is because it aims to be a revision tool to illustrate essay writing technique.

Remember that the quality of your ideas is more important than how many pages you write. This may come as a surprise, but a new report reveals that it is often the case that top band answers are just 2-2½ sides of quality analysis. Your focus should therefore be on analysing and exploring ideas in detail.

The essay provides just one example of a response to an exam question. Some students might include other ideas and different examples to illustrate their points. English literature is an interesting subject because characters and themes can be interpreted in a variety of ways—it is possible for students to write completely different responses and be awarded the same mark.

To access the higher marks, planning is essential: I would recommend brainstorming your ideas in a plan and noting whether they are language, structural or contextual points (if your exam board assesses context). When you write your essay, begin with the most important points.

Five minutes before the end, stop! You should have covered the most important points, and you cannot write about everything. Use the remaining time to read through your essay:

- If your exam board rewards accurate spelling, punctuation and grammar, you need to proofread: the difference of one mark could affect your grade if you are on the borderline. (*Mr Bruff's Guide to Grammar* is a useful resource, available in hardback on Amazon or as an ebook on www.mrbruff.com .)

- Have you analysed language and structure?

- Have you used context to inform your analysis?

- Have you shown awareness of form by talking about Orwell's intentions and using vocabulary such as *novella, character and chapter*?

ESSAY TITLE:

Explore how Orwell uses the character of Squealer to present ideas about power in *Animal Farm*.

PLAN

1. Introduction: his function in relation to the power of words (& context)
2. Orwell encourages the reader to mistrust the power of words—significance of his name
3. Use of propaganda to exert power--'milk and apples':
    - Pseudo-science & situational irony—context, power of Soviet propaganda
    - Language analysis—connotations & greediness of pigs
    - Incident structured at end of chapter
4. Power to rewrite history (context—Spain & Soviet Union). Thought control.
5. Power of the written word: changing commandments and reactions. Cyclical nature of tyranny. Link to context.
6. Absolute power (Boxer's death) and the reaction of the animals
7. Conclusion: power of words ➔ unused power of a passive population.

ESSAY

Through the character of Squealer, Orwell illustrates the power of words to manipulate and control others. Squealer is presented as Napoleon's mouthpiece, and he serves as a Minister of Propaganda: his historical counterpart is Molotov, Stalin's head of communist propaganda. Squealer might also represent the Soviet newspaper *Pravda*, which was used by Stalin for propaganda purposes. Squealer is therefore aligned with power through what he says and his position as a member of Napoleon's inner circle.

Through his presentation of Squealer, Orwell encourages the reader to mistrust the power of words. For example, Squealer's name suggests the squealing of pigs, and Squealer is defined by his ability to vocalise; however, the onomatopoeic verb *squeal* is an unpleasant, shrill sound, suggesting that his propaganda, however unwelcome to the ears, has the power to be heard. Informally, *squeal* can mean to protest or complain. Squealer vigorously defends Napoleon's decisions, protesting any dissent from the animals. Squealer's words, however unpleasant to the ears, have the power to be heard and cannot be ignored.

Orwell shows how propaganda is a tool of power through Squealer's explanation of the pigs' theft of the 'milk and apples' at the end of chapter 3. Squealer employs pseudo-science to justify the actions of the pigs when he deliberately confuses the animals with the 'Science' of the benefits of the 'milk and apples' to the pigs who, he claims, are working for the good of the animals. We have situational irony because the reader becomes aware that the 'All animals are equal' ideology is breaking down and that the pigs are beginning to elevate themselves to a privileged class. This is reflected in history when the Soviet Union propaganda machine used language to justify luxury for the ruling classes. The reader knows that 'milk' nourishes, so the theft heightens reader awareness of the pigs' self-interest. Furthermore, the 'apples', which are also full of goodness, connote the apple on the tree of knowledge in the Garden of Eden, thereby suggesting temptation and sin. By employing the plural noun 'apples', Orwell shows the greediness of the pigs, foreshadowing that their temptation to seize power and sin against the other animals will grow. By placing Squealer's explanations (or propaganda) at the end of the chapter, Orwell encourages the reader to reflect upon the power of Squealer's words, the flaws of communism and the impact that his propaganda is having upon the gullible animals.

Orwell also exemplifies the power of propaganda to rewrite history through Squealer's use of lies. For example, he announces in chapter 7 that Snowball fought against the animals at the Battle of the Cowshed. The animals believe the pigs, despite some of them having taken part in the battle and knowing better. When Orwell was a resistance fighter in Spain, he similarly noticed that some newspapers inaccurately reported historical events such as battles or chose not to report them at all. In the Soviet Union, Stalinists distorted historical facts to suit their purposes; for example, the Stalinist regime altered photographs by removing images of people who fell out of favour. Orwell uses Squealer to draw attention to the practice of rewriting history and to illustrate that by controlling information, the pigs have the power to direct the thoughts of the animals.

As the novella progresses, Orwell associates Squealer with the power of the written word to draw the attention of the reader to the cyclical nature of tyranny. The reader has seen the Seven Commandments change to suit the purposes of the pigs; then, in chapter 8, the animals find the unconscious Squealer next to a broken ladder with a paintbrush, yet they do not challenge the evidence in front of their eyes that Squealer has broken the ideology of 'Animalism' by rewriting the Seven Commandments. From the animals' reaction, we see Squealer's power to manipulate written language to increase the pigs' status and the benefits. In the Soviet Union, Stalin and other high-ranking members of the communist party also enjoyed the privileges of the tsar, so Orwell's use of Squealer alerts the reader to the fact that tyranny is cyclical: contrary to the principles of Animalism, one tyrant replaces another.

Towards the end of the novella, Orwell demonstrates the absolute power of Squealer's propaganda through the reactions of the animals after Boxer is taken away. Having chosen to ignore the evidence written on the side of the knacker's van that the horse's ultimate destination is a glue factory, they instead believe Squealer's lies about the high levels of care that the dying Boxer received. We are aware that the dogs have been used to threaten and kill the animals, so perhaps the animals choose to believe Squealer out of fear. Another reason might be that it makes them feel better to believe Squealer's lies because the alternative, the reality of his death, would mean that they must examine their consciences. At this point in the novella, we see how easy it is for Squealer to manipulate the thoughts of the animals, animals who have the power to challenge the pigs but who do nothing.

To conclude, Orwell employs the character of Squealer to encourage the reader to evaluate the propaganda used in the Soviet Union. He also encourages the reader to consider the power of words to manipulate and to control. He also draws the attention of the reader to the animals' inability or unwillingness to see that they are being lied to; this encourages the reader to reflect upon the nature of a passive population that allows corrupt regimes to rise to power.

Printed in Great Britain
by Amazon